Walter Brodie

PITCAIRN'S ISLAND,

AND

THE ISLANDERS,

IN 1850.

By WALTER BRODIE,

AUTHOR OF "THE PAST AND PRESENT STATE OF NEW ZEALAND."

TOGETHER WITH EXTRACTS FROM HIS

PRIVATE JOURNAL,

AND

A FEW HINTS UPON CALIFORNIA;

ALSO,

THE REPORTS OF ALL THE COMMANDERS OF H.M. SHIPS THAT HAVE TOUCHED AT THE ABOVE ISLAND SINCE 1800.

Rediscovery Books

Reproduced by kind permission of the
Royal Geographical Society

Published by
Rediscovery Books Ltd
Unit 10, Ridgewood Industrial Park,
Uckfield, East Sussex,
TN22 5QE England
Tel: +44 (0) 1825 749494
Fax: +44 (0) 1825 765701

This edition © Rediscovery Books Ltd 2006

To find out more about Rediscovery Books
and its range of titles visit
www.rediscoverybooks.com

Published in association with

Royal Geographical Society
with IBG

Advancing geography
and geographical learning

The **Royal Geographical Society with IBG** was founded in 1830 to advance geographical science. Today it supports geographical research, promotes geography in schools and through outdoor learning, in society and to policy makers. Geography connects us to the world's people, places and environments.
The **Rediscovery Books** series allow us to see how previous geographers and travellers understood and recorded the world.

In reprinting in facsimile from the original, any imperfections are inevitably reproduced and the quality may fall short of modern type and cartographic standards.

Printed and bound by Lightning Source

PREFACE.

In the month of March, 1850, I happened to be left upon Pitcairn's Island, the vessel from which I landed having been blown off the island during the night. Four other gentlemen, fellow-passengers, were likewise in the same predicament with myself, our worldly possessions consisting of the clothes we stood up in, whilst the chances of our being able to pursue our journey within any reasonable time were quite uncertain. Thrown thus upon the hospitality of the islanders, avowedly destitute of the means of making them any return, we were not only received with the most cordial welcome, but treated with a *prévenance* of attention (the offspring of natural politeness) which could not have been exceeded in the most polished European society, and which enables me, in spite of the disappointed object of my voyage, to reckon those few weeks among the happiest of my life. My time was principally occupied in gathering materials for an account of this virtuous and interesting community, which I feel myself bound to make public, in hope that it may draw attention, now more than ever needed, to their condition, and thus partially discharge the obligation which my fellow-passengers and myself have incurred.

WALTER BRODIE.

DIARY.

MARCH 23rd, 1850. At 10 P.M. sighted Pitcairn's island twenty-five miles to the westward of us, scarcely visible. But for the moon, which was immediately above it, I do not think we should have seen it. This island is memorable as affording a refuge to the mutineers of H. M. S. *Bounty*. Our captain thinking it advisable to procure some water if possible, bore up for the island, having only 700 gallons of water fit for drinking on board. During the night we dodged about under easy sail to windward of the island.

March 24th. Sunday, at daylight we found ourselves off the settlement, which is on the north side of the island, but for some time no notice appeared to be taken of us on the island. At 8 A.M. we saw a red flag hoisted near the precipice in front of the settlement; tacked ship and stood in towards the island, when we perceived a boat coming from the shore under sail, which proved to be a whale boat with nine islanders in it. After going through the usual ceremonies of putting innumerable questions to each other, we prepared to go on shore. The captain asked them to get some water off immediately; but they objected to do so, as it was Sunday, telling him, however, that if it were a matter of necessity, they would bring him off a little, which they did, about 180 gallons during the day. They all strongly recommended the captain to anchor, as several vessels lately requiring water had done so; but he told them it was too much trouble hauling up the chains and bending them, a trouble which he might easily have overcome in about half an hour, as they were quite handy. The fact is, there was a sort of supercargo on board, who appeared to have more to say about it than the captain, and who ultimately carried his point in not anchoring the vessel. Had the captain acted in a manner which he thought would have benefitted the owners, and not have listened to the opinions of a boy, who knew as much about his supercargoship as he did about the expediting of the vessel, he would have saved much time and expense. At 10 A.M. the islanders took their departure to procure the water, and the ship's boat went on shore—the captain, Mr. Webster, Mr. Carleton, Mr. Taylor, and myself, with an islander to pilot us through the surf to the landing-place. Upon landing we were met by a few islanders, the remainder being at church. After conversing with them at the landing for some twenty minutes, the captain made up his mind to remain off the island under easy sail until the next day, to enable him to complete his watering, and to procure fruit, potatoes, &c., &c. We then made a start for the settlement, ascending a very steep hill at an angle of forty-five degrees, which was very slippery after the rain, which fell very heavily in the morning, the first that had fallen here for two months. After climbing about 200 feet, and then getting over a stile, which was placed to prevent the cattle from approaching the settlement, we came to the market-place, a small open space surrounded by cocoa-nut trees; and a few hundred yards farther, came to the village, to which the inhabitants have not at present given a name. It is very prettily placed, with a lovely view of the sea between the trees. In passing the church we found that the service had only just commenced. I proposed accordingly that we should join in it, and in a few minutes we were all in prayer among the islanders. Upon our going into this neat little church, the congregation did not appear so full of curiosity as might have been expected; hardly any so much as turned round to see whom we were like. During the service the marriage ceremony was performed between two young persons, who seemed rather bashful on the occasion, which, I presume, was on account of so many strangers being present. Lydia Young and Daniel M'Coy were the names of the happy couple. After church was over, we all congratulated the happy couple, and shook hands with every one, which took some time. After introducing ourselves to Mr. Nobbs, the minister, we proceeded to his house, where we ate some fruit, and then took a walk about the island. About 3 P.M. one of the islanders reported that our vessel, the barque *Noble*, had carried away her fore-yard, which we thought strange, as there had been but little wind during the morning; but which still might have been possible, as we had sprung it badly before arriving at Pitcairn's Island. After a short time, however, we saw the vessel under easy sail, showing no signs of any mishap. After our walk, our captain and Mr. Supercargo left a list of articles required for the *Noble*, which the islanders promised to take off on the morrow. They then took their leave of us all, as they intended sleeping on board the barque *Noble* that night. Previous to their leaving us, they both, especially the captain, gave us leave to remain on shore all night, in presence of nearly all the islanders, stating at the same time that they were going to take off an islander with them, of the name of Matthew Quintal, and bidding us be ready to go on board the following morning. We now mustered five passengers on shore, two others having come on shore in a shore boat.

March 25*th*. Strong east wind with rain at times, no appearance of the *Noble*. Employed myself all day in collecting information relative to the island. At 5 P.M. Mr. Carleton, an islander, and myself walked up to the top of the look-out range, which is rather more than 1000 feet above the level of the sea. We looked for some time before we could see any vessel; at last we saw the *Noble* about fifteen miles to leeward of the island, on the starboard tack, trying to gain the island. We wished to get off to her, but the islanders said there was too much wind; in fact, the surf was running so high at the landing-place, that we could not have gone through it.

March 26*th*. Strong breezes from the S.E. and squally with much rain; no vessel in sight, the weather being very thick and hazy. Employed myself as yesterday.

Two stone axes and two stone spear-heads were given me, which had belonged to the natives who had lived upon this island previously to the arrival of the *Bounty*. Mr. Nobbs sent two of his children out into the bush to look for land shells. In the course of a few hours they returned, but with only three sorts, which were all that appeared to have been seen upon the island by any of the inhabitants. I must now mention a circumstance that was told me this day, and which took place on board the ship *Pilgrim*, bound from Auckland, New Zealand, to California, as an illustration of the feeling which prevails among these islanders. The passengers were preparing to go on shore to visit the island in the quarter boat, and very foolishly crowded into her before she was lowered down from the davits. The consequence was that one davit gave way, so that the boat was towed along at an angle of forty-five degrees by the other. Some of the passengers clung to the boat; others who could swim, assisted those who could not. But in the confusion a child was lost sight of, and must have perished, had it not been fortunately observed by one of the islanders just as it was sinking, who immediately jumped off the poop of the vessel, dived after the child, and brought it up safe. The father of the child came up from below with both his hands filled with dollars, which he pressed on the acceptance of the man who had done him so great a service; but without success, for he steadily refused to accept any remuneration for what he considered a simple act of duty. This same man, be it remembered, had come on board for the express purpose of making money by the disposal of his produce, so that the nice distinction which he drew as to the means of acquiring it, deserves to be only the more highly appreciated.

March 27*th*. Fine clear weather this day; it had cleared up about 2 A.M. with a light wind from N.N.W. At noon the vessel was seen from the look-out range, about forty miles to the north-west of the island, standing to the eastward. We were all highly delighted at this news, as we feared yesterday that she might have been blown off; we now expected her close in with the island the next morning, and made the necessary preparations. In the afternoon, Mr. Carleton, John Adams, and myself went to the east side of the island, to try and get to a place where there were some unknown characters, supposed to have been cut into the solid rock by the original inhabitants of the island. It was called the Rope—a rope having been used in former days to descend the precipice. Upon our arrival at the edge of the perpendicular cliff, we did not like the look of it: it was a very dizzy height of nearly 600 feet perpendicular; broken necks would have been the inevitable consequence of missing a single step. Adams strongly dissuaded us, on account of the slippery state of the ground, from attempting it; we, therefore, returned home again with disappointed curiosity. On our way home we visited the height called St. Paul's, which is the north-east point of the island, and from which we again saw our vessel.

March 28*th*. Fine clear weather, with a light north

wind, which increased at noon to a moderate breeze. At daylight we were all on the *qui vive*, expecting to see the *Noble* close in to the island; when, to our surprise, we found that she was about twenty miles to the northward, still standing to the eastward. On looking at her through the glass (there being two excellent ones on the island), she appeared to have no foresail, fore-topsail, or fore-top-gallant-sail set, but all her head-sails set. As the sun was shining upon her, we could see her very distinctly. Our observations all agreeing relative to her sails, we came to the conclusion that she must be fishing her sprung fore-yard, or repairing whatever damage she might have sustained on the Sunday, supposing the native report, already mentioned, to have been correct. From her situation, we, of course, assumed her to be the *Noble;* but from the course she was steering, I thought it probable that she might have had no sail on her foremast yesterday, and that, instead of her sailing towards the island during the night, she had actually drifted so much nearer to us, by making lee-way. As the wind was likely to come from the eastward, I thought she intended to get well to the eastward before she came down to take us on board, as she was in a partially crippled state. At 10 A.M. she was a little to the eastward of the island. At 11 A.M. we all proposed going off to her in whale boats belonging to the island. The islanders would have willingly pulled us out, although to so great a distance, had she showed any inclination to wait for us. But no such inclination was displayed; and as the wind was now increasing, it would have been folly to think of catching her. At noon the wind veered to the south-east, when she steered to the north-east, and in about an hour was out of sight, leaving us totally unable to account for her proceedings. My own opinion is, that she remained by the island until Tuesday night, when the weather appeared very unsettled, and the captain thinking there was no chance of beating to windward in such a hulk of a vessel, shaped his course for California. But previously, I have no doubt that Mr. Webster (better known as a shopman behind the counter at Gibson and Mitchell's retail store in Auckland) had urged him to pursue this course; at the same time giving him (the captain) an instrument in writing, exonerating him from any blame or expense attending it, thinking that our expenses in getting away from the island, &c., &c., would be far less than the enormous difference which the detention in trying to make the island might make in the sale of the *Noble's* cargo—a cargo which was partially perishable. Time, I suppose, will explain everything. Should this barque not have been the *Noble,* and the *Noble* have been drifted to the westward by the easterly winds of Monday and Tuesday last, she had now ample time for regaining her lost ground by the N.N.W. and N. winds, which had been blowing for many hours. But my firm belief is that the vessel we saw this day was the barque *Noble,* and that she steered for California on Tuesday night; and that, after steering some few hours to the northward, she met with the northerly winds, which compelled her to steer to the eastward, when she again came most unwillingly in sight of the island. From her position last night, and also this morning, she must have been close hauled, or nearly so, and must have made about four points lee-way, being a very dull sailer; and having no square sails on her foremast, she must have drifted bodily to leeward during the night. I have no doubt that, at daylight this morning, they were much surprised on board the *Noble* at seeing their position, but could not prevent our seeing them; and that, as they must have made up their minds to leave us, they did not think it worth their while to come down for us, which would not have detained them three hours, or, at the utmost, four hours. It is possible that they did not imagine that we saw them so clearly as was the case. Here we were, five of us, left upon an island, without a change of clothes or linen, and not a sixpence in our pockets; but, luckily for us, left, perhaps, with little doubt, upon the most moral and religious island in the world, and amongst the most kind-hearted, hospitable, and generous islanders ever met with. Hearing that there was another road to the hieroglyphics, rather more circuitous than the one we attempted yesterday in vain, and not of quite so dangerous a nature, Carleton, Adams, and myself made another attempt to reach them. Upon arriving at the edge of the precipice, it was an awful-looking place to go down; but, if anything, rather more easy to the eye than the other road. The first hundred yards we slid down in a sitting position, on our haunches, having but little regard for the seat of our trousers, a part of which we expected every moment would leave us. We then came to a place, in my opinion, far worse than what we looked at yesterday: it was a ledge of rock, about ten feet long, and of only a few inches in breadth. I must say it made me feel rather nervous; but our guide having told us that it was the worst place we had to cross, I hurried over it as quickly as I could, but with as much caution as possible. Adams persuading us that there was no danger, I did not agree with him. To him it was nothing; he skipped across just like a goat. It is extraordinary to see these islanders go up and down the precipices, and jump from rock to rock, like so many goats. After crossing this bad place, the remainder of our journey down to the sea was still very steep; but, with a few resting-places to recover breath, we reached the sea-shore at last in safety, with no other damage than a few scratches and broken trousers. We then proceeded along the coast for about one-third of a mile. The walking here was very bad, it being over large and loose rocks; fortunately it was low water, or I should have had to swim round a headland that formed one side of the bay—an exercise at which I am not very expert. We now arrived at the spot which had cost us so much trouble and anxiety to reach. The hieroglyphics were carved at from two to ten feet from the ground, many of them appearing to be nearly obliterated. The rock in which they were cut was exceedingly hard, and much resembled the French burr stone. On the opposite page is an accurate representation of what we saw—the moon, the sun, the stars, a bird, figures of men, &c., &c. After remaining about an

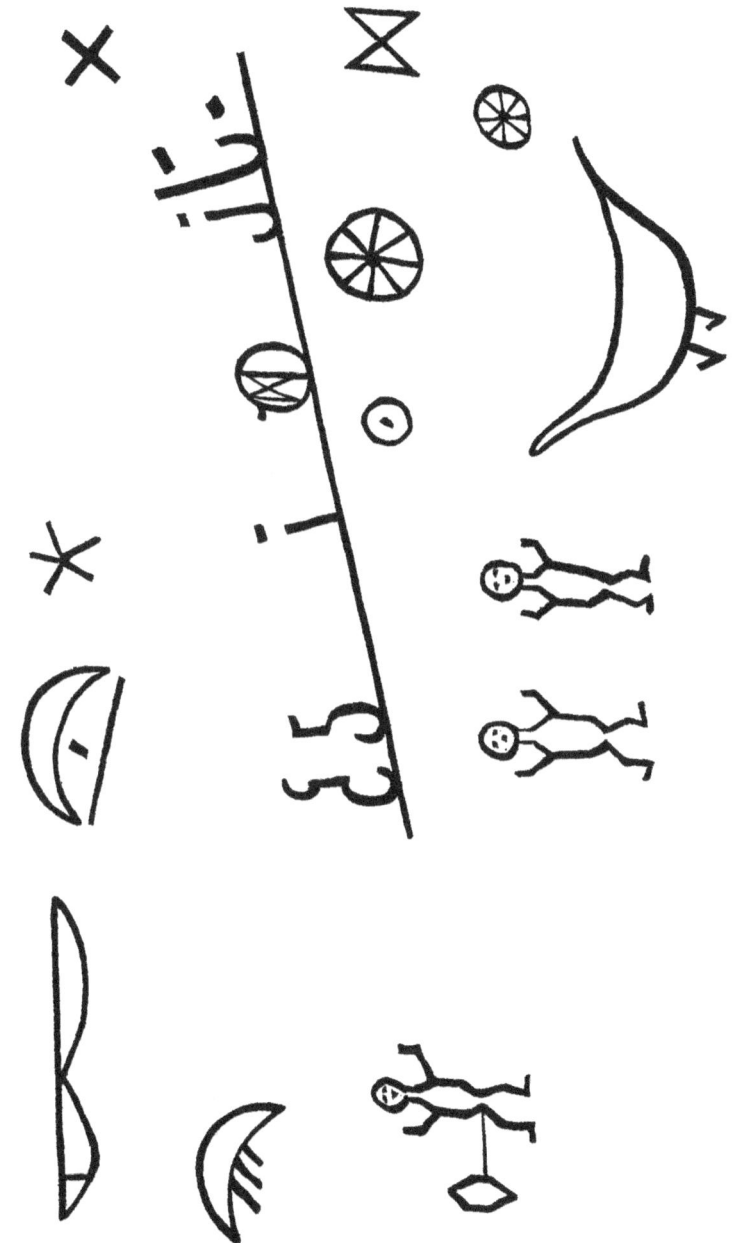

hour, we returned home; not by the same way we came, but by the road which we attempted yesterday, which made a difference of nearly a mile in shortening the distance. Adams took the lead, with a rope and a hoe in his hand, making holes in the ground and soft rock, wherever they could be made to our advantage, in ascending this anything but delightful ascent. When nearly up to the top of the first ridge, I squeezed myself between two rocks to rest, and then requested Adams to pass the rope down to fasten round my waist, as immediately above me the rocks were perpendicular; and having a rope, I thought I might as well make use of it. Adams then hauled, or I should say assisted, me up this difficult pass. Carleton would not use the rope, preferring his own hands and feet to the assistance of others. Upon arriving here, which was the place we looked down upon yesterday, I was most thankful. How curiosity could have tempted me to undertake so dangerous an excursion, I know not; but I do strongly recommend Europeans never to attempt the same for the sake of curiosity. The only strangers that ever attempted and accomplished it besides ourselves were Dr. Domet, Lieutenant M'Leod, and Mr. Lock, of H.M.S. *Calypso*. These figures can be visited in a canoe or boat; but only in very fine weather, on account of the great surf running on that side of the island. In the evening there was no appearance of any vessel in sight. I myself gave up all hope of the barque *Noble*, but the others did not, thinking that she had gone to Elizabeth Island to procure a spar for a fore-yard. Elizabeth, or Henderson's

Island, is about 120 miles from Pitcairn's—latitude, 24° 0' 2" south; longitude, 124° 45' west—is larger than Pitcairn's, and covered with timber of only a small size, similar to that with which the houses are built upon Pitcairn's, and which is nearly all used up. Not long ago, eleven of these islanders, along with John Evans (one of the three resident Europeans), were carried to Henderson's, or Elizabeth Island, in an American whaling vessel, on an exploring expedition. The landing was anything but good, and the soil not near so rich as that of their own island, being of a much more sandy nature. Water there appeared to be none; but, after a long search, they found a fresh-water spring below high-water mark. Some cocoa-nuts, which had been purposely carried there, were planted upon the best ground they could find. Several goats had been likewise shipped for turning out, but were actually forgotten until some time after they were returned on board. They were only a few hours on the island, and, therefore, were unable to form or give any detailed description of it. Elizabeth Island is of a peculiar formation, very few instances of which are known; viz., dead coral, more or less porous, elevated in a flat surface, probably by volcanic agency, to the height of eighty feet. It is five miles in length, one in breadth, and thickly covered with shrubs, which makes it difficult to climb. It was called Henderson's Island after the captain of the ship *Hercules* of Calcutta, though first visited by the crew of the *Essex*, an American whaler, two of whom landed on it after the loss of their ship, and were subsequently taken off by an English whaler, who heard of their fate at Valparaiso. They are very anxious to procure a small vessel or large boat, of about twenty tons burden, to enable them to visit this island at pleasure, and bring off house-timber as required, as likewise to convert it into a run for their live stock; thus relieving their little island from that burden, and enabling them to direct the whole of its capabilities to the use of man. They have established a sort of Bank amongst themselves, in which a large part of the money paid by vessels for refreshments, is suffered to accumulate for the purpose of purchasing a small vessel.

March 29th. Good Friday. This day is the only fast observed here during the year. There are two services in the church. Wind from N.N.W. to N.N.E. and fine clear weather. Much talking among the islanders regarding the *Noble* and our situation. They are greatly annoyed at young Quintal's being taken away in the vessel. It is curious that this same Quintal has repeatedly spoken when at home of his great desire to visit California, provided that he could be blown off the island in some vessel, so as to spare him the pain of taking leave of his friends and family. I certainly never saw family ties so closely drawn as they are here.

March 30th. This day I was shown two-guns (nine-pounders), one large copper boiler, several pegs of iron kentledge, part of an armourer's bellows, an anvil, two sledge hammers, and a quantity of loose copper, which came out of the *Bounty*. Moderate north wind during the day. Employed myself in collecting information regarding this island, as also in collecting shells, which were not very numerous. Took some lessons in tappa-making, under Mrs. Nobbs and her married daughter's tuition. It being a very noisy process I did not remain long a scholar at my lesson. The tappa cloth is used by the islanders in place of sheets. Before they received presents from the British Government in clothing, &c., &c., they used it for their ordinary clothing. This day my tobacco was reduced to only one pipe full, which to me was the greatest possible deprivation. In the evening Mr. Nobbs found a stick of tobacco in his medicine chest, which I accepted from him as a very great prize. Nearly all the men here smoke, but there is not more than half a pound of tobacco upon the whole island. This day an unfortunate accident was discovered. The bull which had been imported by H. M. S. *Daphne* was found dead, having fallen over the rocks, the soft ground having given way under its weight.

March 31*st.* Moderate east wind, with fine clear weather. Went twice to church and attended the Sunday-school.

April 1*st.* Wind and weather as yesterday. This day a general meeting was held in the church, to take our case into consideration, the result and minutes of which we did not hear. Papers were also signed by the majority of the islanders who were present when Captain Parker gave us all leave to sleep on shore, promising at the same time to take us all off the next morning, and also by those islanders that particularly watched the *Noble* on the 21st ultimo. Viewed the remaining

relics of the *Bounty*. A new house having been built
for John Adams, which had never been occupied, Carleton proposed that we should all go into it, and keep
house for ourselves, so as to relieve our individual hosts
from our maintenance, although we should still be dependent upon the community for an occasional basket
of yams, &c., &c. We all agreed but one (Baron de
Therry) to Carleton's proposal; as such an arrangement
would likewise make us more independent, and enable
us to keep our own hours without disturbing any one,
as well as allow our hosts and hostesses to take possession of their own sleeping apartments, which they had
given up to us from the time we came on shore. Our
hosts would not listen to our keeping house for ourselves, neither did they at all like our sleeping out of
their houses. But after a good deal of battling, we agreed
to take our meals with them as usual, which was the
only way by which we could compromise the matter.
I then told Mr. and Mrs. Nobbs that they must give up
treating me as a guest, and allow me to live just like
themselves, in their ordinary way. I offered to assist
him in his plantations, which he appeared rather hurt
at. I shall not forget a remark that Adams (the elder)
made to Carleton, when he offered to work in his plantation. He said, " that now he had three times more
pleasure in seeing him in his house than before; for that
while the ship was there he might have supposed that
he looked for some return, whereas now it was quite
clear that he could make none." They appeared to
rack their ingenuity in trying to put us at our ease, and

to make us believe that the advantage was upon their side, and that with a delicacy and natural good breeding which it was refreshing to witness. Towards evening oranges, pine-apples, bananas, plantains, &c., &c., came raining in upon us, together with two large bags of new clothes, voted at the meeting, into which we were to dive, and appropriate whatever happened to fit. took one shirt, one pair of trousers, and one underwaistcoat, which was all I required. Shoes and stockings being luxuries, I did not meddle with them. I should have mentioned that a few days ago Carleton commenced teaching the whole of the adults upon the island to sing, at which they were highly delighted. At 8 P.M. Carleton gave an extra singing-lesson in our new house, which ended in a house-warming. Edward Quintal brought his fiddle; he had picked up some hornpipe and reel tunes by ear on board ship, which he really played with great spirit, and the true artistic twang, not omitting the stamp and wriggle, or the grind upon the fourth string. Some of the islanders danced very well, not waltzes certainly, but reels. The women never dance. We three, Carleton, Taylor, and myself, danced a Scotch reel, which threw the spectators into ecstasies. The women shrieked with laughing. We ended with blind-man's-buff and many other innocent games, in which the ladies joined: there was every sort of sky-larking possible.

April 2nd. At two o'clock in the morning we sent the whole island home—certainly not to sleep. Fine clear weather, with moderate south-east wind. During the morning I employed myself in making some walking canes from the cocoa-nut and palm trees; in the afternoon I went down to the rocks, and helped the men and women to carry up some planks, which were being landed in their boat from another part of the island. Dined with Arthur Quintal, senior; attended the school and received a copy-book containing the writing of many of the scholars, which I had specially requested.

April 3rd. Fine weather, with light north-east wind. Collected much information from A. Quintal, senior, which will appear verbatim in my description of the island.

April 4th. Fine, north-east wind. Employed all day collecting shells, but not with much success.

April 5th. Wind south-east, and fine. Employed myself in collecting shells; took a good look out from the highest part of the island, thinking to see a vessel.

April 6th. North-west wind, and fine. Made some walking canes, and attended the musical class.

April 7th. North-west wind, and fine. Went twice to church.

April 8th. North-east wind, and fine. Finding so much to do in collecting information regarding the island, I was compelled to leave off attending the musical class. Cleaned up all my shells excepting a duplicate set.

April 9th. Wind south-east, and fine. After breakfast, about fifty of the islanders went round to the west side of the island in their three whale boats, and some in canoes, to bring in a store of cocoa-nuts. I joined them, and a very pleasant day I spent. I was much disappointed at not finding any new specimens of shells, as it was by far the warmest side of the island. Cocoa-nut trees on the west side of the island are very abundant, and appear to do much better there, on account of the warmth. In cultivating this tree, nuts which are perfectly dry and ripe are chosen, and put into a piece of ground by themselves. As soon as they begin to shoot, they are taken up and planted where they are intended to remain. This plan is adopted in consequence of many of the nuts failing to germinate; they generally take eight years before they bear; a good tree in full bearing will produce from 100 to 300 nuts annually. In the course of conversation with some of the girls, whilst feasting upon cocoa-nuts, I spoke to them about their beauty; when one of them observed she did not think I was an Englishman. I asked with some curiosity what could have led her to such a conclusion, and was informed by the fair damsel in question, that I flattered too much to be British born. I was not a little surprised at the answer I received.

April 10*th*. Strong south-east wind, and fine. At daylight a vessel was observed, which created a great commotion on the island, more especially among the women, who thought there was some chance of their losing their singing-master (Carleton); many of them were in tears, and many more in very low spirits. At 10 A.M. I went over to the south side of the island with Mr. Nobbs, who took a spy-glass with him; but it was some time before we could make her out, as she was about ten miles to the southward of the island. After remaining about an hour we returned. At 1 P.M. she came in sight of the settlement. I took another look at her through the glass, and found her to be an American whale ship, but no chance of her being near enough to board until the morrow. When the islanders heard me say she was a whale ship, and not an English merchantman, as many of us thought, from her coming from the southward, the delight that appeared in the whole of their countenances was most gratifying to us. In fact, they had begun to look upon us, not as strangers who had been left upon the island, but as of themselves.

April 11*th*. Strong south-east wind. At 8 A.M. the captain of the American ship came on shore. She proved to be the *George and Susan*, of New Bedford, Captain White, eleven days from Tahiti, and bound on the middle ground. He expressed great commiseration for our mischance, and said that had he been bound to the Sandwich Islands or Tahiti he would willingly have taken us on; but as he was away for his whaling ground he could not offer us any assistance. He gave us some Californian news, and among other things happened to mention, in the hearing of some of the islanders, that lime juice was worth sixty dollars a barrel. The islanders immediately set to work with the intention of filling a few barrels for us, that we might not be entirely unprovided for in case we should arrive at San Francisco before the *Noble*, which it must be confessed would be placing us in a most awkward predicament. Our intention is to indulge them with the satisfaction of giving it to us, to take it on, and remit the proceeds to the donors. At noon, the church bell was loudly rung. I ran to learn the occasion, and found that a barque with English colours flying was close to the island. This really created a very great sensation, as there could be but little doubt of the stranger being bound for California, from the number of people that appeared to be on board. The poor women, if it were possible, looked far more melancholy than they did when the former vessel was reported in sight; but as to ourselves we were too gladly anticipating the chance of getting off the island, to follow out the intentions and pursuits which we had originally planned in New Zealand. But at the same time I must say that I shall much regret when I do leave, on account of the great kindness I have received from every one on the island. Their kindness and real hospitality have been unbounded, and I firmly believe that I often hurt their feelings by not accepting everything that they offered me. At 3 P.M. seven of the islanders went off to the English barque in their whale boat, and I accompanied them. At 4 P.M. we boarded her, when she proved to be the barque *Colonist*, from Adelaide viâ Auckland, Captain J. Marshall, with 120 passengers, three months out, and short of provisions. After remaining on board for some time, I informed the captain of our unfortunate (although in one sense of the word fortunate) situation, and begged very hard to obtain a passage from him, which he said was quite out of the question, on account of the crowded state of his vessel. Putting all things together, I really thought that his answer would have been mine, had I been placed in the situation that he was; but, however, being a married man I thought it was my duty to try to the last, which I did, and was again refused. The want of water and provisions appeared to be the great stumbling-block to any of us getting a passage in the barque. I therefore offered to get the islanders off to the vessel the next morning early, to water the vessel and procure whatever provisions could be spared. About 5 P.M. I left the vessel, along with the seven natives, in the whale boat, anticipating a more fortunate result in the morning. Upon landing, I was assailed by a storm of questions as to our chances of getting away, which I was unable to answer, for I did not know what they were myself. In the evening while talking to Carleton about the vessel I mentioned the captain's name; he immediately recognised him as an old acquaintance, having once chartered his former vessel (the Haidè, since lost in the Bay of Honduras), for the purpose of bringing cattle from Sydney to New Zealand. This I looked upon as rather a lucky coincidence, and that Carleton and myself had a better chance of now getting away than we had before. During the evening, I packed up every thing that I had upon the island, which certainly was not much, so that I might at all events be ready.

April 12*th.* At 8 A.M. we went off in one of the island whale boats. As soon as Carleton got on board the *Colonist*, he went up to Captain Marshall and shook hands with him. Captain M. at first did not recognise him; but very soon did, and, as may be supposed, was much surprised to find his old acquaintance upon such an out of the way island. After breakfast we both asked Captain Marshall if he could not make room for us, as neither of us was a Daniel Lambert, nor were we encumbered with much baggage. He again told us that he had no room, and that his people were on short allowance already. The islanders then asked us if we were ready to go on shore with them, as they were ready to go. Carleton looked at me and I looked at him. I was impelled to petition the captain once more to make room for us, when he again denied us; but with some little hesitation, which I took advantage of, and offered to put provisions on board for ourselves, if he would only make room for us. He looked down the hatchway of the fore cabin and said—" If you can manage to sleep there, you may go," pointing to the lockers where we were to sleep. We both thanked him, and most willingly accepted the kind offer. We then returned on shore, taking with us a Mr Carwardine, one of our intended messmates, whom we looked upon in the light of a hostage, insuring us against the departure of the vessel while we should be making our adieus. Many of our kind and dear friends met us upon our landing, seemingly afraid to ask what success we had met with. Our boat's crew relieved us from the unpleasant task of communicating the news ourselves. It will be some time before I forget the pretty faces of some of the women, their cheeks covered with tears when they were made aware of our intention of leaving them, which they said was very unkind upon our part; I told them it was our duty to take the first opportunity which presented itself; but that we should never cease to bear them in mind. One of the boat's crew had heard me speak to the captain about bringing some provisions on board for our own use, which he mentioned forthwith to those on shore. One and all set to work without delay, and collected for us as much as filled a large whale boat, pigs, goats, ducks, fowls, pines, oranges, lemons, bananas, plantains, and cocoa nuts, along with two large sacks of sweet potatoes and yams. Owing to the almost immediate arrival of the *Colonist*, the islanders were unable to execute their provident intention with regard to the lime juice, and we shall lose the pleasure of surprising them in the manner we had anticipated. After taking leave of my worthy host, Mr. Nobbs, and also of Mr. Buffett, who did not accompany us to the landing-place, we all, I may say the whole population, proceeded to the place of embarkation. Before leaving, Mr. Nobbs paid us both a very high compliment relative to our moral and sedate behaviour while resident upon the island; indeed we had both of us made a point of never being out after dark, to obviate all chance of remarks being made, and which the natives had not been slow to observe. I may here mention a matter in which the islanders take the greatest interest, of which I have made hitherto but little mention, purposely that I might wait the issue of the experiment. As might be supposed, our great anxiety was to make some little return for the warm hospitality with which we were treated; a wish however which it was not so easy to gratify, seeing that our sole possessions, when we found ourselves left on shore, consisted of the clothes we wore and a tuning-fork which happened to be in the baron's pocket. It luckily occurred to my friend Carleton, who had observed their imperfect attempt at psalmody in church, that a little musical instruction might prove a great amusement to them. Our worthy friends caught at the proposal with eagerness; and on the very same day all the needful apparatus—a ruled board, conductors, baton, &c.,—were prepared, and the first lesson was given to the whole adult population, in a new house as yet unoccupied. They proved remarkably intelligent, not one among the number being deficient in ear, while many had exceedingly fine voices. The progress surpassed the most sanguine expectation of the teacher; on the fourth day from the commencement, they sang through a catch in four parts, with great steadiness; for people who had been hitherto unaware even of the existence in nature of *harmony*, the performance was very remarkable. Both pupils and preceptor appeared to take equal delight in the task; and we heard them, after a fortnight's instruction, singing among themselves in the open air trios and quartettos, for the most part performed in chorus, during the greater part of the night. They have among them some books of instruction in this delightful art, and are now sufficiently advanced to be able to pursue the study without assistance. It is very gratifying to leave behind us some little memorial of our residence, even though it be of so airy a nature as this; abiding our time to requite so much kindness with tokens of a more substantial nature. Our situation upon the island was certainly, in a manner of speaking, an unfortunate one; but nevertheless a happy period in our lives, and to have given cause for offence would have been a most foul breach of hospitality. May every one who enjoys the pleasure of a few days' sojourn on the island, be looked upon on leaving with the same respect as we ourselves! I am now going to make what may be perhaps considered a strong assertion, which is, that there never was, and perhaps never will be, another community who can boast of so high a tone of morality, or more firmly rooted religious feelings, than our worthy and true friends the Pitcairn islanders. To have witnessed such a state of things is a blessing that few men and fewer women have ever been privileged to enjoy upon God's earth. The only islanders that I ever saw that at all approached them in one of these respects, is the island of Mauke, one of the Hervy Islands, which I visited in 1842, on my way from Tahiti to New Zealand; an island about four times as large as Pitcairn's, with a population of about 400. They were brought up and taught under a native teacher from Tahiti, some forty years ago, who was taken there by the late Rev. John Williams and the Rev. Mr. Barff, of Hauhine, one of the Society Islands. On this island there were one or two strange women from some of the neighbouring islands, who had committed themselves; but upon Pitcairn's such a transgression was never known since old John Adams's time. A scene followed our arrival at the landing-place, while the boat was being loaded, that I shall never forget.

The poor girls clung round us as we stood upon the beach; but more especially did they cling round my friend Carleton, who had taken so much trouble in teaching them to sing; many of them with the handkerchiefs thrown over their heads, and all of them in floods of tears. We tried to put a bold face upon the matter, but had much ado to maintain that decorous impassibility which is required of men with beards upon their chins. Carleton tried to get up a chorus; but it broke down, and only made matters worse. This scene lasted for about an hour. One of the passengers of the *Colonist* (Mr. Carwardine), who was not in the secret, looked on in mute astonishment; and I am sure that Carleton, as well as myself, felt glad when the signal for embarkation was made by the boatmen. Things having gone so far, we thought we might make a handsome finale to our sojourn upon the island. We first took our worthy hostesses, who were rather ancient matrons, and gave them what was probably the heartiest kiss they had received these many years. The ice once broken, there was no affectation of mock modesty, we went to all in turn, and gave and took in right good earnest: the contrast here was great, as we had hitherto behaved with the most marked reserve; but we parted with the same feelings as if we had been members of the same family.

And thus ends my brief stay among the most simple, innocent, and affectionate people it was ever my lot to be thrown amongst. There is a charm in perfect innocence which he must be indeed hackneyed and hardened who cannot feel. Such a society, so free, not only from vice, but even from those petty bickerings and jealousies—those minor infirmities which we are accustomed to suppose are ingrained in human nature—can probably not be paralleled elsewhere. It is the realisation of Arcadia, or what we had been accustomed to suppose had existence only in poetic imagination,—the golden age; all living as one family, a commonwealth of brothers and sisters, which, indeed, by ties of relationship they actually are; the earth yielding abundantly, requiring only so much labour as suffices to support its occupants, and save them from the listlessness of inactivity: there is neither wealth nor want, a primitive simplicity of life and manner, perfect equality in rank and station, and perfect content. They have happily been preserved from establishing a community of property, which would indeed be a complete bar to civilisation. Add to this, that their practical morality and strong sense of religion promise a lasting continuance of the blessings they enjoy, together with another pleasurable emotion—warm loyalty to their queen and attachment to the mother country; their only anxiety being the smallness of their island. At sunset we got on board the barque *Colonist,* when we found that some of the passengers had just gone on shore, and would not be on board again until morning, so I made myself as comfortable for the night as circumstances would admit of.

April 13*th.* Shortly after breakfast, two whale boats came off with the passengers, and one of the islanders brought Carleton and myself a letter each. The following are copies:—

"To Mr. H. Carleton, Esq.

"*Pitcairn's Island, April* 12*th,* 1850.

"Kind Preceptor,

"When you parted from us last evening, little did we then think that we should be so nigh to you another day, or that we should be able to address you. It would have given us much pleasure to have seen you on shore; but as that may never be, we are glad to have an opportunity of sending you our last and fondest adieus. Wherever you go, our prayers and best wishes will follow you; and, till time lasts, we shall ever think of our beloved preceptor.

"From your loving pupils,

(Signed) "Edward Quintal.   Louisa Quintal.
"Nancy Quintal.   Sarah Quintal.
"Susan Quintal.   Jemima Young.
"Rebecca Christian.   Martha Young.
"Eliza Quintal.   Dorcas Young."

"To Mr. Walter Brodie.

"*Pitcairn's Island, April* 12*th*, 1850.

"Kind Friend,

"Little did we think, when parting from you yesterday, that we should be able to address you again to-day. It would have given us great pleasure to have seen you; but as that may never be, we now embrace this opportunity of sending you our last adieus. We will long think of you; and, wherever you go, our kind wishes will follow you. Remember us to all your friends, and think of us wherever you go.

"Yours most truly,

(Signed)   "Rebecca Christian.
"Sarah Quintal."

At 4 p.m. the two whale boats left the barque *Colonist* for the island; and, when a few yards off from the vessel, they gave us three hearty cheers, which were answered by all on board in the most deafening manner. At 5 p.m. sailed for San Francisco.

Crew of H. M. Ship Bounty, who landed at Pitcairn's Island, December, 1789.

Fletcher Christian	Acting-Lieutenant.
Edward Young	Midshipman.
—— Brown	Assistant-Botanist.
John Mills	Quarter-master.
William M'Coy	Seaman.
Isaac Martin	Seaman.
John Williams	Seaman.
Matthew Quintal	Seaman.
John Adams	Seaman.

The present inhabitants of this island are the descendants of Christian, Young, Quintal, M'Coy, Mills, and Adams; together with three Europeans, Nobbs, Buffett, and Evans, who have been allowed to remain upon the island for upwards of twenty-five years. Brown, Martin, and Williams had no issue; neither had any of the Tahitian men.

FLETCHER CHRISTIAN married Isabella, a Tahitian woman. Issue; Thursday October, Charles, and Mary.

Thursday October married Susanah, widow of Edward Young. Issue; Charles, Joseph, Thursday October, Mary, Polly, and Peggy.

Charles second, married Maria Christian. Issue; Rebecca, Charles.

Joseph, not married.

Thursday October married Mary Young. Issue; Albert, Elias, Alfonzo, Julia, Agnes, and Rose Anne.

Mary, not married.

Polly married Edward Young.

Peggy married Daniel M'Coy; and secondly, Fletcher Christian.

Charles first, son of Fletcher Christian of the Bounty, married Sally, a Tahitian child, that came to the island when an infant, in the Bounty. Issue; Fletcher, Edward, Charles, Isaac, Sarah, Maria, Mary, and Margaret.

Fletcher married Peggy Christian, widow of Daniel M'Coy. Issue; Jacob, Stephen, Nathan, William, Priscilla, Polly, Lucy, Emily, and Abigal.

Edward died unmarried.

Charles married Charlotte Quintal. Issue; Andrew, Gilbert, Kitty, Adeline, Ellena, Cordelia, and Lucy Anne.

Isaac married Mirriam Young. Issue; Henry, Godfrey, and Emiline.

Sarah married George Nobbs.

Maria married, first, Charles Christian; secondly, John Quintal; and thirdly, William Quintal.

Mary married Arthur Quintal, senior.

Margaret married Matthew M'Coy.

Mary, daughter of Fletcher Christian of the Bounty, never married.

EDWARD YOUNG married Susannah, a Tahitian woman. Issue; none; but had a family by two Tahitian women during the time he was married to Susannah, one of which was Fletcher Christian's widow, the other was the wife of one of the Tahitian men. Issue by the former of these two, Edward, Polly, and Dorothea; by the latter, Nancy, George, Robert, and William.

Edward married Polly Christian. Issue; Moses.

Polly married George Adams.

Dorothea married John Buffett.

George married Hannah Adams. Issue; Frederick, Simon, Dinah, Betsy, Jemima, and Martha.

Robert died unmarried.

William married widow of Matthew Quintal second. Issue; Mayhew, Mary, Mirriam, Dorcas and Lydia (*twins*).

Moses married Albina M'Coy. Issue; Mary Elizabeth.

Frederick married Mary Evans. Issue; none.

Simon married Mary Buffett. Issue; Lorenzo, Robert, and Eliza.

Dinah married John Quintal second.

Betsy married John Buffett second.

Jemima and Martha, not married.

―――

— Brown married a Tahitian woman, but had no issue.

―――

John Mills married a Tahitian woman. Issue; Elizabeth, who married Matthew Quintal.

―――

William M'Coy married a Tahitian woman. Issue; Daniel and Kate.

Daniel married Sarah Quintal. Issue; William, Daniel second, Hugh, Matthew, Daniel third, Jane, Sarah, and Albina.

Kate married Arthur Quintal first.

William died unmarried.
Daniel married Peggy Christian. Issue; Philip.
Hugh died unmarried.
Matthew married Margaret Christian. Issue; Russel, Jane, Diana, Mary, Harriott, Sarah, and Sophia.
Daniel third, married Lydia Young.
Jane and Sarah died unmarried.
Albina married Moses Young.

ISAAC MARTIN married a Tahitian woman, but had no issue.

JOHN WILLIAMS married a Tahitian woman, but died without issue.

MATTHEW QUINTAL married a Tahitian woman. Issue; Matthew second, Arthur, Sarah, Jane; he also had a child by Susannah, the wife of Edward Young of the Bounty, Edward.

Matthew married Elizabeth Mills. Issue; John and Matthew third.

Arthur matried first, Kate M'Coy; secondly, Mary Christian. Issue by the first wife; Arthur, Kitty, John, Charlotte, Phœbe, James, Caroline, and Ruth: issue by the second wife; Absolem, Nathaniel, Joseph, Cornelius, and Mary.

Sarah married Daniel M'Coy first.

Jane went to the island of Rurutu, in the brig Lovely Ann.

Edward married Dinah Adams. Issue; William first,

Edward second, Abraham, Henry, Caleb, Martha, Louisa, Nancy, and Susan.

John Quintal, son of Matthew second, married Maria, widow of Charles Christian second. Issue; Eliza, Sarah, Ellen, and Maria.

Matthew Quintal unmarried.

Arthur second, married Martha Quintal. Issue; Edward, Edmund, Victoria, Rhoda, and Rachael.

Kitty died unmarried at Tahiti.

John married Dinah Young. Issue; John, William, Augusta, Matilda, and Kesiah.

Charlotte married Charles Christian third.

Phœbe married Josiah Adams.

James unmarried.

Caroline married John Adams second.

Ruth, Absolem, Nathaniel, Joseph, Cornelius, and Mary, unmarried.

William Quintal, first, married Maria, widow of Charles Christian; secondly, married widow of John Quintal. Issue by the first wife, John, Oliver, Edward, Abbey, and Helen.

Edward second, unmarried.

Abraham married Esther Nobbs; no issue.

Henry and Caleb, unmarried.

Martha married Arthur Quintal second.

Louisa, Nancy, and Susan, unmarried.

JOHN ADAMS first married a Tahitian woman, the widow of John Mills. Issue; Dinah, Rachael, and Hannah. Secondly, the widow of William M'Coy of the Bounty. Issue; George.

Dinah married Edward Quintal first.
Rachael married John Evans first.
Hannah married George Young.
George married, first, Polly Young. Issue; John, Jonathan, and Josiah; married, secondly, widow of Daniel M'Coy. No issue.
John married Caroline Quintal. Issue; Gilbert, Byron, George, and Polly.
Jonathan married Phœbe Quintal. Issue; Calvin and Eliza.
Josiah unmarried.

GEORGE NOBBS married Sarah Christian. Issue; Reuben, Esther, Fletcher, Francis, Jane, Naomi, James, Edwin, Jemima, and Sydney.
Esther married Abraham Quintal; all the rest are single.

JOHN BUFFETT married Dorothy Young. Issue; Thomas, John, David, Robert, Benjamin, Edward, and Mary.
Thomas, unmarried.
John married Betsy Young. Issue; Henry and Eveline.
David, Robert, Benjamin, and Edward, unmarried.
Mary married Simon Young.

JOHN EVANS married Rachael Adams. Issue; John, William, George, Mary, Dinah, and Martha.
John, William, George, Dinah, and Martha, unmarried.
Mary married Frederick Young.

LIST OF CARLETON'S MUSICAL CLASS.

Lydia Young	La	La 2	Mez.	1 or 2
Mirriam Young	La	La 2	So.	1
Louisa Quintal	Si	Sol	Mez.	1
Phœbe Adams	La	Sol	Mez.	2
Martha Young	La	Mi	Con.	2
Albina Young	La	Fa	Mez.	
Mary Christian	La	Mi	Mez.	2
Caroline Christian	La	La	So.	1
Rebecca Christian	Fa	Si	Con.	a 2 or 3
Mary Christian	Sol	Si	Mez.	
Peggy Christian	Sol	Si	Mez.	
Ruth Quintal	Sol	La	Cont.	2 or 3
Mary Young	Fa	La	Mez.	1 or 2
Dorcas Young	Sol	Sol	Mez.	
Esther Quintal	La	La	So.	1
Mary Young	Fa	La	Mez.	2
Eliza Quintal	Sol	La	Mez.	
Maria Quintal	Fa	La 2	Con.	2 or 3
Dinah Quintal	Sol	La	Mez.	
Nancy Quintal	Fa	La	Mez.	a 2
Jemima Young	Fa	La	Mez.	3 or 3
Elizabeth Buffett	Sol	La	So.	1
Charlotte Christian	La	Fa	Mez.	
Susan Quintal	Mi.	Do 2		a
Sarah Quintal	Fa	La	Mez.	a 2
Martha Quintal	Fa	La	Mez.	a 2

Simon Young	La	Do	Full	B
Abraham Quintal	Sol	Do	Full	B
John Evans	Si	Re	Thin voice	
Thomas Buffett	La	Re	Thin voice	t
Thursday Christian	La	Do	Full	B
William Quintal	Si	Fa	Thin	t
John Quintal	Si	Fa	Thin	t
Arthur Quintal	La	Fa	Full	t
Daniel M'Coy	La	Sol	Full	B
Driver Christian	La	Fa	Full	t
David Buffett	La	Do	Thin	
Matthew M'Coy	Sol	Fa	Full	B
John Buffett	La	Do	Thin	
Frederick Young	Sol	Fa	Full	B
Benjamin Christian	Si	Fa	Thin	t
William Evans	Sol	Mi	Thin	t
Robert Buffett	Do	Do	Thin	t
Philip M'Coy	Sol	Mi	Full	B
Samuel M'Coy	Sol	Mi	Thin	t
Moses Young	La	Do		
Fletcher Christian	La	Sol	Full	B
Isaac Christian	Si	Ra	Thin	
Jacob Christian	La	Do	Full	B
James Quintal	Sol	Do	Full	B
George Adams	Sol	Do	Full	B
Charles Christian	La	Do	Full	
Josiah Adams	La	F	Thin	t
Jonathan Adams	Si	Do	Thin	t
John Buffett, sen.	Sol	Sol	2	t
Edward Quintal	La	Fa		t
John Adams	Sol		Full	B

LANDING IN BOUNTY BAY.

PITCAIRN'S ISLAND,

Now memorable for having afforded refuge to the mutineers of H.M.S. *Bounty*, was discovered by Cartaret. It is about one mile and a half long, and four and a half in circumference. The true latitude and longitude, incorrectly laid down in many charts, is 25° 0′ 4″ south, and 130° 0′ 8″ west. It it rises abruptly from the sea, and is iron bound. It was taken possession of, November 29th, 1838, by Captain Elliott of H.M.S. *Fly*, for the crown of Great Britain. On nearing the island, vessels should make the north-east end, St. Paul's Point,* off which run a few large rocks, all above water; the largest of these is a square basaltic islet, and inshore are several high pointed rocks, which the pious islanders have named after the most zealous of the apostles, about fifty feet above the water, with room for a boat to go between them and the mainland. About a quarter of a mile to the westward, is a small boat harbour, the only landing-place which a stranger would find without the assistance of an islander, the surf appearing to break heavily all round the northern end of the island The *Bounty*'s crew pulled twice round the island, before they hit upon it. There is very good anchorage, when

* The highest point of land in the accompanying print in Bounty Bay there is any easting in the wind, for vessels of any size, to the westward of the island, about a quarter of a mile to the southward of the north-west end of the island, off which lie a few large rocks above water, similar to those off the north-east end, the depth of water being from eight to twenty-five fathoms from a quarter to three quarters of a mile off shore. There are neither shoals nor sunken rocks off the island, over a quarter of a mile off shore. For the last fifteen years the regular trade-winds have ceased to blow; but, seven months out of the twelve, the winds are from south-east to east (from September to March inclusive). In the bight of the first little bay, after rounding the north-east end of the island, and about a quarter of a mile to the westward of the same, you will observe a small clump of cocoa-nut trees (six in number), very near the water's edge, on the right hand, and one single cocoa-nut tree on the left, about two hundred yards from the six trees on your right, with a large grove of cocoa-nut trees above on the hill, a little to the westward. When near the shore, three boat-houses may be observed, containing as many whale boats and several canoes. The landing-place is just below the boat-houses, and between the clump of one and six cocoa-nut trees—a shingly beach, only of sufficient breadth to allow of two boats abreast to land at one time. Care must be taken to observe the rollers, which are very irregular in coming in, and the channel in is winding between the rocks. These rocks are only a few yards from the shore, and the distance between them very narrow. When a stranger comes in, a native generally takes his station upon a rock on shore, and waves his hat, to indicate a favourable opportunity for pushing ahead; but strange boats seldom come on shore before some of the natives go on board them. A stranger, in a square-sterned boat, might meet with an accident; but, at the worst, a sound ducking would be the only consequence. To any person acquainted with the locality, I consider the landing as perfectly safe. Having set foot on shore, you ascend a steep hill, almost a cliff, for about three hundred yards, to a table land, planted with cocoa-nut trees, which is called the Market-place; about a quarter of a mile beyond which, at the north end of the island, lies the settlement, flanked by a grove of cocoa-nut trees, kumeras, and plantains, &c., &c., which makes the approach very picturesque.

The island is evidently of volcanic origin. The highest point (Look-out ridge) is about 1008 feet above the sea. Scoriæ are scattered about, but not to an extent to interfere with cultivation. The soil generally is of a deep red, apparently decomposed lava, and very productive. The island rat, which is rather small, and the lizard, are the only quadrupeds indigenous to the island. Only one land bird is known to breed upon the island— a small species of fly-catcher, of a dirty white and brown colour, and three sea-birds—a white skiff (which is referred to in the laws), a brown skiff, and the man-of-war bird or hawk, all of which the islanders eat. They have three whale boats: two of them were presented by the English Government, the other was purchased from a whaler. Their canoes, about twenty in number, hold generally two persons, and are so light that one man can carry them. They can be made to last five years, by being constantly painted; but the tree from which they are made, is getting very scarce. The culinary vegetables are kumeras, potatoes (Irish and sweet), yams, pumpkins, and two sorts of beans which they keep and dry for many months. Cabbages and onions are rather scarce. Herbs they have none. Their fruits are pines, four species of plantains, and bananas, oranges, limes melons, paw-paw apple—a fruit somewhat resembling a small English apple, and cocoa-nuts. St. Pierre, in his book upon the works of nature, mentions that he never heard of any accident occurring from the fall of a cocoa-nut from off the tree during his lifetime, or even ever read of such a thing; but one of these rare—I may say very rare—occurrences happened here lately, and nearly killed Mrs. Nobbs. The indigenous *Flora* of the island is not rich, but many valuable trees and plants have been imported from Tahiti. Of land shells there are only three species, and those very minute. Of sea shells I collected about forty species; but many more are probably to be found, as I was only able to search a part of two sides of the island, having been obliged to take advantage of the arrival of the barque *Colonist*, before completing my exploration. There are but few insects to be seen; but at certain times the caterpillars are very destructive, making their appearance in large swarms. There are but four head of cattle upon the island. H. M. S. *Daphne*

Captain Fanshaw, in August 1849, landed a bull and cow from Valparaiso: the cow has since calved; but the bull was unfortunately killed, as mentioned in my diary. Two heifers and a young bull were sent by some gentlemen from New Zealand as a present; but, on account of the tedious voyage, the captain of the vessel in which they were shipped, found it necessary to kill one, that fodder enough might be left for the other two. Owing to contrary winds, he was obliged to run into Tahiti, where the cattle were reshipped on board an American whaler, the master of which very kindly gave them a passage to their destination. I observed many goats running wild, and about a score of rabbits around the houses, which were brought by H.M.S. *Daphne* in 1849. Fowls are very numerous. Pigs scarce. Cats numerous, and wild in the bush, and are encouraged to kill the rats, although they probably destroy more fowls than rats. There are many dogs, useless animals enough, and very currish in appearance.

There is no doubt but that this island was formerly inhabited, although the native race must have been extinct many years prior to the arrival of the *Bounty*. Burial-places are still to be seen, and large, flat, hewn stones, in different parts of the island, which must have been for pavement in front of their houses, such as are still in use among other tribes in the South Seas. These stones, when observed by the crew of the *Bounty*, had very large trees growing up among them, by which in many places they had been displaced. Stone images were likewise found, supposed to have been objects of worship; they were made of a hardish coarse red stone. Stone spearheads and small axes are very common; and round stone balls, of about two pounds' weight, some of which are generally found when working up new ground, all of which are made of a bluish black stone, very fine grained and smooth. The spots where the images and stoneware were made, may be recognised by the large accumulation of chips in various parts of the island. Human bones have been repeatedly found, although not during the last eight years; and, in one instance, a perfect skeleton was discovered, in the last state of decay, with a large pearl shell, of a sort not belonging to the island, under the skull. This is a custom with the natives of the Gambier Islands, Bow Island, High Island, Toubouai, and nearly all the Pumutu or Low Islands. The cocoa-nut trees, bananas, plantains, and breadfruit trees, as well as the yams and sweet potatoes, found here by the crew of the *Bounty*, are an additional sign of the previous occupation of the island, more especially as they were confined to one single spot. It is very unlikely that these plants should have been indigenous so far to the southward, as they will not grow upon every part of the island, but merely upon a few of the warmest spots or situations on the lower ridges. These aborigines were most probably drifted here upon a raft, it having been a custom, many years ago, especially at the Gambier Islands, which are to the w.n.w., about three hundred miles from Pitcairn's Island, and of many of the Low Islands, to put those who were vanquished in war upon rafts, when the wind was off the land, sending them adrift to whatever place they could fetch. Two actual instances of this practice were mentioned to me by Mr. Nobbs; one came under his cognisance while he himself was at the Gambier group. There is an island, about sixty miles to the E.S.E. of Gambier Island, called Crescent Island, to which Mr. Nobbs and Captain Abriel, in the American schooner *Olivia*, and Captain Cornish, in the *Olive Branch*, paid a visit in 1836, having heard that pearl-shell was to be found there in great abundance. On landing, they were much surprised at finding about forty natives living upon it, although unknown to the natives of the Gambier Islands. There being a few of the Gambier islanders on board of the *Olive Branch*, the party was enabled to communicate with these people, who told them that their prior generation, who were then all dead, had been put upon a raft and sent to sea, having been worsted in a battle at the Gambier Islands; and that after drifting upon the ocean for several days, they were cast on shore where they were now found. After remaining upon the island for two days, Mr. Nobbs's party returned to the Gambier Islands, taking with them a few of the Crescent islanders. On their arrival at the Gambier group, the natives of that group, hearing of the strangers, a great meeting was held, when it was ascertained that the account which had been rendered was perfectly correct. The next day some of the Gambier group chiefs hired Captain Abriel's launch, giving him in payment four tons of Too (Breadfruit put under ground, after being cut up and left there to ferment). This was much required by Captain Abriel, who had a party of natives fishing for pearl shells, as food for his divers. The launch started, and in a few days returned again with all the Crescent islanders on board. Upon their landing, the Gambier islanders gave them a grand feast, of which the guests partook so plentifully, that some of them actually died from repletion. In the other instance mentioned by Mr. Nobbs, the beaten party, likewise from the Gambier Islands, reached an inhabited island, called Rapa or Opazo, about 700 miles s.s.e. of Tahiti, or 600 miles s.w. from the Gambier Islands. The last of these refugees died about six years ago.

Very little information is at present to be gathered upon the island, concerning the famous mutiny of the *Bounty*. Beyond a few stray anecdotes of no great interest little remains. But the account given by the islanders, such as it is, differs materially from that published by Captain Bligh, after his return to England. They flatly deny his assertion, that the original cause of the mutiny was the connexion formed by the crew, while at Tahiti, with the Tahitian women; attributing it entirely to his own perverse temper and tyrannical conduct. His language, particularly to his officers, is stated to have been habitually and inexcusably coarse. Of this a single example will suffice, which I give in the words of the narrator. "Some fruit, which had been sent on board for the captain's cabin, having been left upon the quarter-deck, disappeared; Captain Bligh was exceedingly angry, and in rating Christian about the matter, made use of this expression, 'I suppose you have eaten it yourself, you hungry hound!'" Can we be surprised at insults of this nature rankling in the mind of a susceptible man, and driving him at last to the desperate deed by which he secured himself against their continuance? After the mutineers put Captain Bligh out of the *Bounty* into his boat, along with seventeen of his crew, the mutineers made sail for the Island of Toubouai, which is about 500 miles south of Tahiti, where they agreed to remain and establish themselves, provided the natives, who were numerous, were not hostile to their purpose. Of this they had very early intimation, an attack being made upon a boat which they sent to sound the harbour. They however effected their purpose, and the next morning the *Bounty* was warped inside the reef that formed the port, and stationed close to the beach. An attempt was made to land, but the natives disputed every foot of ground with spears, clubs, and stones. After two days they returned to Tahiti, and were received with the greatest kindness by their former friends. After some time they again returned to Toubouai, but were again obliged to go back to Tahiti, finding the natives there opposed to their settling among them. After landing, Haywood and fifteen others of their party were taken by H. M. frigate *Pandora*, which was sent out in search of them as soon as Bligh returned to England, and which vessel was wrecked in Torres Straits, on her way to England. Christian and eight others then sailed for Pitcairn's Island, after securing for themselves each a wife, as well as six Tahitian men and three women, wives of three of these six men, Christian keeping his own counsel as to their destination. He resolved upon Pitcairn's Island, induced by Cartaret's discription, which had chanced to be on board the *Bounty*. Although many notices of the mutineers and their descendants have at different times been given to the world, I do not recollect to have seen any connected history of so interesting a community; for the simple reason, that no one has ever remained on the island long enough to obtain it, previous to my stay there. Its early records are sad indeed. The crimes of the original settlers were heavily visited upon them, as will appear by the following account, taken down verbatim—even to the grammatical errors—from the recital of Arthur Quintal, senior, who, with George Adams and five women, are all that remain of the first generation :—

" When the *Bounty* came here, there were nine Englishmen, six Tahiti men, twelve Tahiti women, and a little girl, landed. The Englishmen had each a Tahitian women for a wife, and three of the Tahitian men were married to the remaining three women. Some time afterwards Williams's wife died of sickness. The Englishmen then combined together, and took one of the Tahitians' wives for another wife for Williams. This created the first disturbance between the English and the Tahitians. William Brown was sent out by the English Government in the *Bounty*, as gardener, to look out after the breadfruit plants, which the said vessel was to convey to the West Indies. Brown and Christian were very intimate, and their two wives overheard, one night, Williams's second wife sing a song,—'Why should the Tahitian men sharpen their axes to cut off the Englishmen's heads?' Brown and Christian's wives told their husbands what Williams's second wife had been singing. When Christian heard of it, he went by himself with his gun to the house where all the Tahitian men were assembled. He pointed his gun at them, but it missed fire. Two of the natives ran away into the bush— one of them to the west part of the island, the other to the south end of the island. The Tahitian (Talalo) who went to the west side, was the husband of Williams's second wife. One day Talalo saw his wife, and the wives of the other Tahitian men, fishing; he beckoned to her, and she went to him. He then took her away into the bush. Another Tahitian, named Temua, then joined Talalo and his wife in the bush. After this, Christian and the other Englishmen sent a Tahitian (Manale) in search of them; he was not long away before he found them, and then returned and told the Englishmen of it. The Englishmen then consulted among themselves what to do, when they agreed to make three puddings and send them. One pudding, having poison in it, was to be given to Talalo, and the other two were to be given to the wife of Talalo and the Tahitian (Temua) who had joined them. The puddings were sent by the native, Manale, who gave them to the three natives individually; but a suspicion coming across Talalo's mind that his pudding had poison in it, he would not eat it, but eat his wife's pudding along with her. When Manale found that Talalo would not eat his pudding, he induced the three to go up into the bush a little way, where he told them he had left his wife among some breadfruit trees. As they went up to see Manale's wife, the foot-path being very narrow, they walked behind each other, Manale being behind and next to Talalo. Manale, having a pistol with him, and having instructions to kill Talalo before he returned, now took the opportunity, and pulled the trigger of his pistol, it being pointed at Talalo's head; but it misfired. Talalo, having heard the noise occasioned by the trigger being pulled, turned round, and saw the pistol in Manale's hand. Talalo then ran away and Manale after him; they then had a severe struggle, when Talalo called to his wife to help him kill Manale, and Manale told the woman she must help him kill her husband, which she did; and in a very short time Manale and Talalo's wife killed Talalo. Manale, the woman, and the other native (Temua), then returned to the European settlement. Williams then took the woman again for his second wife, as he had formerly done. Christian and the other Englishmen then sent Manale to find the other Tahitian (Ohuhu), who had gone to the south side of the island, whom he also soon found, and then reported his success to the Englishmen. The English then sent Manale and another Tahitian (Temua) to kill him, which they succeded in doing, while pretending to cry over him. They then returned home again to the Europeans. The whole of the *Bounty* people then lived together for some time (about ten years) in perfect harmony. The six Tahitian men from the *Bounty* were brought down as servants to M'Coy,

Mills, Brown, and Quintal. This island, when these people came here, was completly covered with sea-birds, and when they arose, they completely darkened the air. These remaining four natives were employed to work in collecting a lot of these birds for their masters' food, after they had done their work in their masters' gardens; they also fed their pigs which they brought from Tahiti on these sea-birds. Whenever the Tahitians did any thing amiss, they used to be beaten by their masters, and their wounds covered with salt, as an extra punishment. The consequence was, that two of these Tahitians, Temua and Nehou, took to the bush, and with them each a musket and ammunition, with which they used to practise firing at a target in the bush. Edward Young had a garden some little distance from the settlement; and the two natives which took to the bush, used at times to come and work for him, as well as the other two natives, who lived in the settlement. Young appeared to be very friendly with the Tahitians; and John Adams mentioned that he had every reason for supposing that Young had instigated the natives to destroy the Englishmen, excepting himself (John Adams), Young wishing to keep Adams as a sort of companion. At planting time, each Englishman had his own garden, which were some distance apart from each other, being in separate valleys, on the north end of the island. Three of the Tahitians, finding that the whole of the Englishmen were widely scattered and unprotected, commenced to destroy them, beginning with John Williams and Fletcher Christian. At the time they shot Christian, Christian hallooed out. Mills, M'Coy, and Manale, were then working about 200 yards from Christian's garden, and M'Coy hearing Christian call out, 'Oh dear!' told Mills he thought it the cry of a wounded man; but Mills thought it was Christian's wife calling him to dinner. After the three Tahitians had killed Christian, they then went to where Mills was working, and one of them (the other two being concealed in the bush) called to Mills, and asked him to let his native, Manale, go along with them to fetch home a large pig they had just killed. Mills then told Manale that he might go. Manale then joined the three Tahitians, when they told Manale that they had killed Williams and Christian, and wanted to know how they might destroy Mills and M'Coy. It was at last agreed that these three men should creep into M'Coy's house, unobserved; which they succeeded in doing. Manale then ran and told M'Coy that the two natives that had taken to the bush were robbing his house. M'Coy then ran to his house, and as soon as he got to the door, these three natives fired upon him, but did not kill him. Manale, seeing that they had not killed him, seized him; but M'Coy, being the strongest of the two, threw him into the pig sty, and then ran and told Mills to run into the bush, as the natives were trying to kill all the white men. But Mills would not believe that his friend Manale would kill him. M'Coy then ran to tell Christian, but found that he had been murdered already. About this time, M'Coy heard the report of a gun, which he supposed had killed Mills, and

which turned out to be the case. M'Coy then ran to
Christian's wife, who was at her house, and told her
that her husband had been killed. Having been confined
that day she could not move. M'Coy then ran to
Matthew Quintal, and told him to run into the bush.
Quintal and M'Coy then took to the bush, and Quintal
told his wife to go and tell the other Englishmen what
had happened. While she was going along she called
out to John Adams, who was working in his garden,
and asked him why he was working this day, she
thinking that he had heard of everything that had
taken place. Adams did not understand her; she said
no more, but went away, without telling Adams anything about the murders. The four natives then ran
down to Martin's house, and finding him in his garden,
ran up to him and asked him if he knew what had been
done this morning. He said 'No.' They then pointed
two muskets at his stomach, and pulled the triggers,
and said 'We have been doing the same as shooting
hogs.' He laughed at them, not suspecting anything the
matter; they then immediately recocked their muskets
and again pulled the triggers. The muskets going off
the second time, Martin fell wounded but not killed.
He then got up and ran to his house, the natives following him; when they got hold of one of the Bounty's
sledge hammers, which they found in his house, and
beat his brains out. They then went to Brown's house,
and found him working in his garden. They fired at him
and killed him. Adams, hearing the report of the guns
when Brown and Martin were killed, went to see what

was the matter. When he arrived at Brown's house he
saw the four natives standing leaning on the muzzles
of their guns, the butt of their muskets being upon the
ground. Adams asked them what was the matter. They
said '*Mamu!*' (silence). They then pointed their guns
at him, when he ran away, the natives following him;
but he soon left them behind. He then went into
Williams's house, with the intention of getting some
thick clothes to go into the bush with, when he discovered that he had been killed. He however took some
thick clothes from the house, and returned to his own
house round by the rocks. He then took a bag from his
own house, and whilst putting some yams into it to
take into the bush, he was fired upon by the natives,
and a ball passed in at the back of his neck and came
out of the front of his neck. He then fell; when the four
natives approached him and attempted to kill him with
the butt end of a musket; but he guarded himself with
his hand, and had one of his fingers broken by so doing.
After struggling for some time, he managed to get
away, and ran off and the natives after him. When
he had got some distance a-head of them, the natives
cried out for him to stop, which he refused, saying
that they wanted to kill him. The natives then said,
'No, we do not want to kill you; we forgot what
Young told us about leaving you alive for his (Young's)
companion.' Adams then went to Young's house with
the four natives, and found Young there. The natives
then went into the mountains, armed, to try and find
M'Coy and Quintal, and after several days' search they

found them along with Quintal's wife, in M'Coy's house, which was up the mountain. When they found them, they were all asleep. The natives fired upon them, but did not wound any of them. They then took to the bush again. After this the four natives returned to the settlement again. One evening, when Young's wife was playing upon a fife, Manale, one of the other natives being present, became jealous at Temua's singing to Young's wife. Manale then took up a musket, and fired at Temua, which only wounded him. Temua immediately told the woman to bring him a musket to shoot Manale. Manale in the mean time reloaded his musket, and shot Temua dead. The two other natives then became much annoyed, and threatened to kill Manale. Manale then took to the bush, and joined Quintal and M'Coy; but they would not have anything to do with him until he put his musket down, which they took possession of. He then told them of what had taken place, and said that he had come to join them and be their friend. Manale then persuaded Quintal and M'Coy to go down with him to the settlement, so that they might kill the other two Tahitians. When within a few yards of the house where the natives were, Manale saw the two natives, and sprang upon the stoutest of them. Quintal and M'Coy, thinking it a scheme of Manale's to entrap them, made off for the bush again; but such was not the case. Manale soon after joined M'Coy and Quintal. Adams and Young then wrote them a letter, and sent it by Quintal's wife, to persuade them to kill their new friend, Manale;

which they succeeded in doing, by shooting him with
his own gun, which he gave them when he went to make
friends with them. After this, the two remaining Tahitians again went in search of M'Coy and Quintal,
when they found them under a tree. They fired upon
them, but did not wound either of them. They again
ran away from the natives, and, whilst running, M'Coy
cut his foot with a piece of wood. The natives seeing
the blood, thought they had wounded him, and then went
home and told Young they had wounded M'Coy. Young
then sent his wife and Martin's widow round to find
M'Coy and Quintal, and to see if either of them were
wounded. Young told his wife to tell them that on a
certain day they all intended to kill the two remaining
Tahitians, and that a certain signal would be made to
that effect. These two women then returned, and told
Young that neither of them were wounded. The plan
was now arranged to kill these other two natives, in
the following manner:—Young persuaded Brown's
widow to go to bed with Tetihiti, the most powerful of
the two Tahitians, and cautioned her on no account to
put her arm under the Tahitian's head when she went
to sleep, as his wife intended to cut his head off with an
axe as soon as he went to sleep. When Young's wife
had killed this Tahitian, she was to make a signal to
her husband to fire upon the other Tahitian, by shoot-
him with his musket; but during the time that Young
was loading his musket, the young Tahitian told Young
to double load it, the young Tahitian thinking that
Young was going out to shoot M'Coy and Quintal.

Young answered, 'Yes, I will.' Young's wife then struck the stout Tahitian in his bed, but did not hit him fair. The stout Tahitian, upon getting up in his bed, was struck a second time with the axe, which killed him dead; at which time she told her husband to fire, which signal he obeyed, and blew the young Tahitian's head nearly off his shoulders. Thus ends the tragedy of the Tahitians. The signal was then made to M'Coy and Quintal to come down, as the two Tahitians were killed; but they would not believe it. Young then cut the hands off the two dead Tahitians, and sent them up by some of the women to M'Coy and Quintal, as a sort of certificate that the two Tahitians were really dead. Upon the women delivering the hands to them, M'Coy and Quintal then descended the mountain, along with the women, and reached the house of Young in safety. They all now remained upon friendly terms for some time. Young took two of the widows into his house (Williams and Christian's) and three children; Adams took Mills's widow and two children, and the widows of two of the Tahitian men; M'Coy took Brown's widow, and Quintal took Martin's widow, into their houses. Adams and Williams lost their wives previous to this bloody tragedy, in 1793. Young was a half West Indian, born in St. Kitts. Whilst there he learned how to make spirits. By his knowledge of making them there he soon made them here, out of the ti-root, by the aid of a large copper boiler which came out of the *Bounty*. The consequence was, that they all took to drinking at times, and many quarrels ensued. Quintal, about this time, lost his wife, she having been killed by falling over the rocks, while searching after birds' nests. Quintal, after the loss of his wife, wanted to marry another one, but the rest of the white men were against it. He then threatened all their lives. Soon after this they got him to drink, and made him intoxicated, when the three Europeans killed him with an axe. After this, M'Coy drank to excess. At times he used to be away from home for a week, and no one knew where he was gone. At last he fastened a large stone round his neck and jumped into the sea, where he was drowned. The day previous to M'Coy drowning himself, Young died of asthma. Adams was now the only man upon the island. The women and children all looked up to Adams with great respect, and always called him father. About ten years after, Adams had a most extraordinary dream, which was, that the angel Gabriel came down from heaven and warned him of his danger for his past wickedness. From this time Adams became a most religious man, and used every act and means in his power to instruct the women and children then upon the island in reading and writing, and in the fear of of God. At this time, Adams always had morning and evening prayers—the only books that were upon the island, at this time, being a few Bibles and Prayer Books. While looking over the Prayer Book one day, he found that Ash Wednesday and Good Friday were fast days, and, at the same time, thought that every Friday and Wednesday were fast days also; and, as such, he kept them until 1823, when Mr. Buffett arrived among them to reside as schoolmaster, and told him of his error. He gave up the Wednesdays as fast days some time previous to his death, which the inhabitants were very glad of, as their hard labour, and two strict fast days a week, did not agree with them. Many of them frequently fainted for want of food; but Friday was kept as a fast day until his death. The only fast day now kept is Good Friday. The manner in which the children first learned their prayers is rather strange. Adams wanted a piece of ground broken up to plant some yams in, and he engaged two young men, Edward Quintal and Robert Young, to do the same for him; and, as payment, a small phial of gunpowder was to be given. After the ground was all broken up, and the yams planted, these two young men asked Adams which he would like to do best—give them the gunpowder, or teach them some prayers out of the Prayer Book: Adams, who was much pleased with this remark, consented at once to teach them, and offered them the gunpowder, which they refused to take from him. Adams told them that, if there were any more of them who would like to be taught, he would teach them. The consequence was, that the whole of them came to him, much to old Adams's delight. The Lord's Prayer and Creed Adams taught them first, immediately after his dream of the angel Gabriel's appearance."

From this time forward a picture, of an opposite character, is presented to the eye. We now gladly turn away from scenes of crime and folly to record the history of the most innocent and well-organised community that has perhaps been ever seen on earth—one, moreover, which assumed this character by a change so sudden, and so contrary to all likelihood, that a direct interference of Providence in its favour would seem the only reasonable manner of accounting for the change. The immediate cause of it, at all events, was the dream already mentioned in Arthur Quintal's recital, by which old John Adams was visited. It startled him much, and led him into a train of serious thoughts; but the recurrence of another vision, of similar character, in which he thought that he was carried away to view the flames and torments of the bottomless pit, completed the work that had been already so auspiciously begun; and his whole remaining term of life was devoted to the expiation of his earlier errors.

In 1799, Adams and Young were the sole survivors out of fifteen males that landed upon the island. They were both, and more particularly Young, of a serious turn of mind; and it would have been wonderful, after the many dreadful scenes at which they assisted, if the solitude and tranquillity that ensued, had not disposed them to repentance. During Christian's lifetime they only once read the Church service. They now, however, resolved to have morning and evening family prayers, to add afternoon service to the duty of the Sabbath, and to train up their own children, and those of their late unfortunate companions, in piety and virtue. In the execution of this resolution, Young's education enabled him to be of the greatest assistance; but he was not long suffered to survive his repentance—he died of asthma in 1800, and Adams was left the sole survivor of the misguided and unfortunate mutineers of the *Bounty*. The loss of his last companion was a great affliction to him, and was for some time most severely felt. It was a catastrophe, however, that more than ever disposed him to repentance, and determined him to execute the pious resolution he had made, in the hope of expiating his offences. His reformation could not have taken place at a more propitious moment. He nevertheless had an arduous task to perform. Besides the children to be educated, the Tahitian women were to be converted; and as the example of the parents had a powerful influence over their children, he resolved to make them his first care. Here, also, his labours succeeded. The Tahitians were naturally of a tractable disposition, and gave him less trouble than he anticipated. The children also acquired such a thirst after scriptural knowledge, that Adams, in a short time, had little else to do than to answer their inquiries, and put them in the right way. As they grew up, they acquired fixed habits of morality and piety, which merit wholly belonged to Adams, and tends to redeem the former errors of his life. He taught himself—so say the islanders—to read. He gave himself up to the study of the Bible and Prayer Book, and devoted himself, during the remainder of his time, in imparting the knowledge which was thus acquired. He was listened to with attention, being now the only male survivor of the *Bounty*'s crew, and looked up to by the half-castes of the first generation with patriarchal reverence. His efforts were crowned with complete success; the morals of the community became as strict as they had heretofore been loose. Religious observances were insisted upon, even to severity of discipline; and the death-bed of John Adams, the mutineer and manslàyer, was cheered by the consolatory reflection that his labours had borne fruit—that the seed which had been sown by him had now struck such deep root as to give the fairest promises of permanently maintaining its title to the soil in which it was laid.

> HE DIED MARCH 5TH, 1829, AGED 65.

In 1795, a ship was observed close in with the island; at the sight of which the mutineers were so much alarmed as to hide themselves in the bush. When they came out again from their concealment, they found that a party had actually landed from her, as was proved by the discovery of a jack-knife on a rock by the sea-side, and some cocoa-nut shells. Their habitation, however, appeared to have remained unnoticed. The first vessel by which the refugees of the mutineers of the *Bounty* were discovered, was the American ship, *Topaz*, Capt. Folger, in 1808. Capt. F. carried away a chronometer and compass, for the purpose of forwarding them to the Admiralty. Whether they were received, or not, I cannot say; but at all events, no notice was taken of the discovery until 1814, when H. M. S. *Britain* and *Tagus* arrived in search of the U. S. ship of war, the *Essex*, which had

From a Sketch by Cap.ⁿ Beechey

John Adams

Ætat. 65.

Maddey lith. 3 Wellington St Strand

been taking many of our whaling vessels. Adams was very much alarmed, very naturally supposing they had come to fetch him away. He did not attempt concealment, but presented himself to the captain, who assured him that they had not come to arrest him—observing at the same time, that it would now be a cruelty to take him away: both on account of the lapse of time that had expired, and the dependence upon .him in which the islanders were placed for counsel. In 1830, the islanders received a present from the English Government, of clothes and agricultural implements, which were brought out *viâ* Valparaiso, by Capt. Hon. Waldegrave, in H.M.S. *Seringapatam.* In 1831, they were removed by the British Government to Tahite.

"H.M. Sloop *Comet;* Port Jackson,
"May 26th, 1831.

"Sir,—I have the honour to report to your Excellency the proceedings of H.M. sloop under my command, since the 5th of last November, when I communicated to you my intention of putting to sea, upon the arrival of the Colonial barque *Lucy Anne,* from Norfolk Island. That vessel arrived in this port on the 4th of December, and was immediately got ready for sea, with all the arrangements deemed necessary by His Excellency the Governor and myself for proceeding to Pitcairn's Island, for the removal of its inhabitants, or such of them as were desirous of removing. I put to sea with the *Lucy Anne* in company, on the 27th of

December, and arrived at the Bay of Islands, in New Zealand, on the 21st of January. Both ships having completed their water and wood, I put to sea on the 26th, and arrived off Pitcairn's Island on the 28th of February; and being guided on shore by the natives, who came off in their canoes, I landed the same day, and made known to the inhabitants the subject of the expedition. On the second day, I assembled all the heads of the families, and having most fully explained to them that they were perfectly at liberty, either to remove to Otahite or remain where they were, I directed Mr. Henry, who was employed by the Colonial Government of the colony to accompany the expedition, to give them every information in his power—which, from his being thoroughly acquainted with the manners and laws of Otahite, as well as being present at the meeting held by the late King Pomare and the chiefs, when the promise of land, protection, and assistance was made to Captain Laws, of H. M. S. *Satellite*, as set forth in his letter to the Secretary of the Admiralty,—he was well calculated to afford. One half of the inhabitants gave me in their names, having resolved to remove to Otahite; and on the following day, the remainder came to the same resolution. The whole immediately commenced making preparations for embarking, by carrying down to the landing-place yams, potatoes, and household goods, which were continued to be embarked on board the ships until the 7th of March; on the morning of which day all the inhabitants were embarked on board the *Lucy Anne*, being eighty-seven in number. I have very great satisfaction in reporting to your Excellency that this service was executed in the short space of four days, the merit of which is entirely due to Lieut. H. F. Peake, of this ship, whose zeal and judgment in directing the embarkation, under the great natural difficulties he had to contend with in the face of a most perilous surf, entitle this officer most fully to this public expression of my acknowledgments. I arrived at Otahite, and anchored in Papiete harbour on the 23rd of March; and found the island, under the government of Queen Pomare, daughter of the late King Pomare, I regret to say, upon the very eve of a civil war; but which, I have great pleasure in making known to your Excellency, terminated by the opposing parties coming to actual hostilities; and that previous to my leaving Otahite, the governors of provinces, and the chiefs opposed to the Queen and her party, having amicably arranged their difficulties, had returned from Papiete to their own provinces, with their numerous armed followers. Although the island was in the most disturbed state on my arrival, I was greatly relieved from the anxiety for the situation in which I was placed with the inhabitants of Pitcairn's Island, by receiving from the Queen and her chiefs on the one side, and the hostile party on the other, assurance that the promises made by her father the King Pomare and them would be most strictly executed. I therefore, at the request of the Queen, landed the people of Pitcairn at the residence of the Queen, about three miles from the anchorage, where houses were provided for them, and at which place they remained until the contending parties returned to their homes; when the Queen gave up for their use a large dwelling, belonging to herself, in the town of Papiete. Previous to their removing to this place, a beautiful tract of very rich land, and belonging to the government of this island, was well examined by the Missionaries, myself, Capt. Walpole, and Lieut. Peake, and determined to be a very eligible territory for their future residence.

"Having made known to the Queen this determination, the Queen assembled the chiefs of the district in my presence, and formally communicated to them that she had assigned this land to the inhabitants of Pitcairn—giving orders at the same time, that her people should immediately commence the construction of houses, when they had made an election of a site suited to their wishes; and the materials for erecting those houses were in considerable forwardness previous to my departure. It will be gratifying for your Excellency to know, that a feeling of great regard was universally manifested to this people by the Otahitians, who endeavoured with great diligence to find out those who were their relatives, in which they were often successful; and in one instance, a woman came a considerable distance, and discovered in one of the four remaining Otahitian women a sister. I have been thus particular in these points, in order to show upon what ground I conclude there is every reason to hope the change from Pitcairn's Island to Otahite will be attended with advantage to them. On my arrival at Pitcairn's Island, I found them exceedingly distressed for water, and what they had was procured with difficulty; and although the fertility of this island has reared a comparatively numerous population, yet this very circumstance, from their increasing numbers, renders the necessity for emigration the more obvious. The gentlemen composing the Christian Mission at Otahite afforded me every service in their power. My thanks are due to Capt. Walpole, of H. M. 39th Regiment, who accompanied me, in the interest he took in the transactions of this voyage, as well as to my officers and crew.

"Hoping that your Excellency will approve of my proceeding,

"I have the honour to be, &c., &c.,
"(Signed)   ALEXANDER SANDILANDS,
"*Commander.*

"To His Excellency, Rear Admiral Sir E. W. C. R. Owen, K.C.B., *Commander in Chief.*"

"Government House, 26th May, 1831.

"SIR,—I have the honour to acknowledge the receipt of your letter, dated at sea the 19th of last month, with its several enclosures, containing an account of your proceedings in carrying into effect the orders of His Majesty's Government with respect to the removal of the inhabitants of Pitcairn's Island to Otahite.

"The manner in which this service has been con-

72   PITCAIRN'S ISLAND,

ducted, cannot fail to prove highly satisfactory to His
Majesty's Government, and I am convinced it will duly
appreciate the benefit which has been derived from
the zeal and judgment with which Lieutenant Peake
performed the duties he was charged with, as stated in
your letter.

"I have only further to express my approbation of
the arrangement entered into with Mr. Bicknell, for
supplying the people removed to Otahite with meat
and vegetables, and to acquaint you that the terms of
the contract will be duly observed, as far as depends
on this Government.

"I have the honour to be, Sir,
   "Your most obedient,
      " and most humble Servant,
"(Signed.)   RD. DARLING.

"Captain Sandilands, R.N., commanding His Majesty's
ship, *Comet*."

A list of the inhabitants of Pitcairn's Island, removed
to the Island of Otahiti, in the New South Wales
Colonial Government barque *Lucy Anne*, under the
convoy of H. M. Sloop *Comet*, Alexander A. Sandilands,
Esq., Commander, March, 1831.

Males' Names.	Age.	Males' Names.	Age.
Thursday October Christian	44	Thursday October Christian	12
Joseph Christian	24	Charles Christian	36
Charles Christian	22	Fletcher Christian	19

A List of the Inhabitants of Pitcairn's Island (continued).

Males' Names.	Age.	Males' Names.	Age.
Edward Christian	18	Matthew Quintal	18
Charles Christian	13	Edward Quintal	30
Isaac Christian	5	William Quintal	13
Moses Christian	Child	Edward Quintal	7
		Abraham Quintal	4
		Robert Young	31
George Adams	25	Mahew Young	4
John Adams	4		
Jonathan Adams	Infants	**ENGLISH.**	
Josiah Adams		John Buffett	—
Edward Young	30	Thomas Buffett	6
Daniel M'Coy	34	John Buffett	4
William M'Coy	20	Daniel Buffett	3
Hugh M'Coy	16		
Matthew M'Coy	10	Robert Buffett	Infant
Samuel M'Coy	Child	G. H. Nobbs	
Daniel M·Coy	19	Ruben Nobbs	Infant
Phillip M'Coy	34		
Arthur Quintal	34	Jack Evans	
Arthur Quintal	15	John Evans	2
John Quintal	10		
James Quintal	5	William Evans	Infant
George Young	34		
Frederick Young	9		
Simon Young	8	Total	48
William Young	32		
John Quintal	20		

Females' Names.	Age.	Females' Names.	Age.
Susannah Christian (Otahitian)		Sarah Christian (or Nobbs)	21
Mary Christian	22	Maria Christian	16
Mary Christian (or Buffett)	2	Rebecca Christian	Infant
Polly Christian	19		
Peggy Christian (or M·Coy)	15	Mary Christian	11
		Margaret Christian	9

A List of the Inhabitants of Pitcairn's Island (continued).

Females' Names.	Age.	Females' Names.	Age.
Polly Young (or Adams)	30	Dinah Young	5
Dolly Young (or Buffett)	33	Betsy Young	4
Mary Christian	37	Jemima Young	Children
Rachael Adams (or Evans)	26	Martha Young	
Sarah Quintal (or M'Coy, sen.)	30	Dinah Adams (or E. Quintal)	29
Jane M'Coy	8	Martha Quintal	7
Sarah M'Coy	Children	Louisa Quintal	2
Albina M'Coy		Betsy Mills (or M. Young)	35
		Mary Young	6
Kitty M'Coy (or Quintal)	30	Marian Young	2
Kitty Quintal	13	*Otahitian Women remaining.*	
Charlotte Quintal	10		
Phœbe Quintal	6		
		Pendence	
Caroline Quintal	Children	Nancy	
Ruth Quintal		Isabella	
		Females	39
Lucy Anne Quintal (born at sea)		Males	48
Hannah Adams (or Young)	30	Total	87

These islanders were supplied with provisions; fresh meat at 3d. per lb., vegetables, 5s. per cwt., by H.M. Government, in a contract made between Capt. Sandilands, on the one part, and Mr. J. Bicknell on the other part, for six months, at the expiration of which time it was supposed they could raise their own provisions.

The provisions consisted of—
  Fresh meat, 3 lb. per week for each man.
  Fresh meat, 1¼ lb. per week for each woman.

Fresh meat, 1¼lb. per week for each child.
Vegetables, 1¼lb. per day for each man.
Vegetables, 1 lb. per day for each woman.
Vegetables, 1 lb. per day for each child.

The superintendence of the above being placed in the hands of Messrs. Pritchard, Nott, and Willton, Missionaries, who were to see the contract fulfilled.

There they were soon visited by sickness, which so rapidly thinned their numbers, that they made up their minds to return without delay; a resolution in which they were confirmed by their dislike of the levity and immorality which surrounded them.

Capt. Freemantle, of H. M. S. *Challenger*, in his report to the Secretary of the Admiralty, dated May 30th, 1830, mentions, that when he arrived at Tahiti, he found that the Pitcairn islanders had left Tahiti, and had returned to their island again, having been assisted by the Missionaries and the Europeans on the island to freight an American vessel, to convey them thither—they being much discontented and unhappy, and a sickness having become prevalent amongst them, which had carried off twelve of their number. " It is an extraordinary circumstance," says Capt. Freemantle, "that many of the copper bolts of the *Bounty*, which had been brought to Otahite from Pitcairn's Island by the islanders, were taken by the master of the vessel as part payment for their freight, to the amount of 200 dollars."

The removal of these people to Tahiti was one of the most unfortunate circumstances that ever befell this community. For a time they were constantly distilling ardent spirits made from the ti-root, and many of them drank to great excess, even after they returned to Pitcairn's Island; but fortunately, in the latter part of 1833, all the stills upon Pitcairn's Island were destroyed, which was a great blessing to every one on the island.

The arrival, in 1828, of George Nobbs, their present teacher and lay minister, I consider to have been one of the providential occurrences in the History of Pitcairn's Island. He was originally in the British Navy, which he quitted for the Chilian service under Lord Cochrane, by whom he was made Lieutenant. On leaving that service, in common with many others he was unable to recover his pay, a considerable sum of which is owing to the present day. He came to Pitcairn's Island, where he has resided, with the exception of a short interval, ever since; combining the duties of a schoolmaster, pastor, and doctor, in the fulfilment of which I must says he is most efficient and indefatigable. His pleasant relations with the islanders were interrupted once, and only once, in consequence of the arrival of a certain Joshua Hill, calling himself Lord Hill, who came from Tahiti in 1832. This man had the art to persuade the simple islanders that he had been sent out by the home authorities as Governor of the island, and certainly beguiled them into the belief of some of the most extraordinary assertions that it is possible to conceive. Indeed, his persuasive powers appear to have failed him but once, and that was in an attempt to seduce them from the Church of England to Wesleyanism, which was steadily resisted. George Nobbs, with the other two European residents, who had seen a little of the world, of course made light of his pretensions, and Joshua consequently declared war to the knife with the malcontents. He then contrived to enlist the majority of the islanders (who I believe were as much influenced by fear of giving offence to the British Government as by any predilection in their new Governor's favour) against them, and forthwith commenced a system of petty persecution which eventually drove all three of the Europeans from the island. George Nobbs and John Evans went to reside at the Gambier Islands, as Missionaries; and John Buffett, the first schoolmaster here, went on to Tahiti. In about nine months' time, however, they received a communication from the Pitcairn islanders, who had now begun to find out their mistake, soliciting their return, accompanied with an offer of paying all their expenses. With this request they complied, and George Nobbs was reinstated as teacher. In 1837 Captain Bruce arrived in H.M.S. *Imogine*, with orders to remove His Excellency, and carried him away to Valparaiso, much to the satisfaction of the islanders, who had become heartily tired of his rule. Previous to the arrival of H.M.S. *Imogine*, I ought to have mentioned, that our friend Joshua gave out that he was a very near relative of the Duke of Bedford, and that the duchess seldom rode out in her carriage without him (*query*—Did he ride inside or outside?). But it unfortunately happened that a few months previous to the arrival of H.M.S. *Imogine*, that H.M.S. *Action* arrived with Captain Lord E. Russell on board, who happened to be a son of the duke; and who was informed by the islanders when they went on board, previous to his Lordship's landing, that the Governor of the island was a near relation of the Duke of Bedford. Lord E. Russell soon found out that Joshua, or the man who rode in the carriage with a duchess, was an imposter, and would have taken him off the island then, had he been authorized; but he could not do it without orders. But reported the case to the Admiral of the station, which was the cause of H.M.S. *Imogine* being sent for him. (See Appendix, for correspondence between Joshua Hill and the islanders with H.M. Government.) In 1839, General Friere, who had known Mr. Nobbs when he was in the Chilian service, landed from H.M.S. *Sparrow-hawk*. I was told that the Chilian Government had put him on board, knowing she was going to Sydney, that Captain Shepherd might treat him as a convict and carry him to New South Wales. To Sydney he certainly went, where he was treated as became his rank; and some time after returned to Valparaiso, probably in consequence of one of those innumerable revolutions by which the Spanish American states have been so long tormented. He promised, *en passant*, to see to the arrears of poor Nobbs, should he ever come into power. From that time to the present there is nothing in the history of the island to relate, excepting what is mentioned in the register at the end of this account—

the surest proof that it must have been peaceful and happy, pursuing the even tenor of its way, untroubled by any of those exciting events which are the main adornments of a tale. But that an important change must shortly take place in their situation is certain; they are already cramped for room, and are living upon a spot of mountainous land, some six or seven hundred acres in extent, being even now unable to supply the vessels which happen to touch with more than sufficient to exchange against the few necessaries with which they cannot supply themselves; and they clearly see that, when this rising generation shall have grown up, emigration will become a matter of necessity. They accordingly feel some anxiety, not unmixed with regret, to leave their present settlement— at least, if they could be removed in a body to some larger island. The Queen of Hauhine (one of the Society islands) has offered to take three families, and give them land as freehold property; which offer was made on account of one of the Tahitian women, who came here in the *Bounty*, having a claim to a large tract of land in that island. Her family name was Puni; she was a Hauhine girl, and happened to be at Tahiti at the time of the *Bounty* leaving for Pitcairn's Island. Puni being dead, of course her offspring, who form a considerable portion of the inhabitants of this island, have a claim to the land of their deceased relative. Many of the most respectable English and American inhabitants, as well as Consul-general Miller at the Sandwich Islands, and also the King, have offered them land there; but their wish is to be located on some island where there are no native inhabitants to interfere with them. If, however, any of them did go to Hauhine, they would find there a most excellent minister, Mr. Barff, who has been there for many years, and whose kindness I shall not easily forget. But, on the other hand, the Pitcairn islanders could not go among a more immoral or loose set of women, than are to be found in nearly the whole of the Society group of islands, unless much altered since I was there in 1842. There was then only too much room for improvement, which I am afraid the French are not likely to have introduced. They, themselves, would much like to go to Juan Fernandez; which, belonging as it does to the Chilian government, I presume is not to be thought of. But it might be procured, should the English Government think proper to remove them there, and without much cost. But should the Home Authorities finally decide upon abandoning Norfolk Island as a penal settlement, which report says there is a chance of, then a more beautiful or suitable location could scarcely be found. At all events, the future prosperity of this interesting people will depend upon the fiat of the British Government; which has already, in smaller matters, taken such interest in their welfare as to lead us to suppose that it will not be neglectful of them, when so important a consideration is presented to its notice. The customs and laws of this community are worthy of attention, more from their being of spontaneous growth, unaffected by any external influences, than on account of anything remarkable or specially curious in themselves. In fact, their primitive simplicity of manner, the absence of vice, the want of scope for the development of any of the more violent passions, naturally induce what may be termed, "a matter of course state of things;" such a state as every one can conceive, and hardly any one has seen. The chief magistrate is elected annually by suffrage, even more universal (pardon the bull) than any thing I have heard proposed at home; all the married people voting, men and women alike, and *all* the single above eighteen years of age. Many might suppose that the honour of the magistracy would be anxiously sought after; but such is not the case. Most of them, to use their own expression, would sooner give the whole community a feast, than be raised to so troublesome a dignity. The duties of that office are onerous; against which there is nothing to throw into the other scale, but the temporary respect in which he is held. He is allowed two councillors, or assessors, to assist him. On the Queen's birthday, which is kept as a public holyday, one of the *Bounty's* old guns is fired, which is very much honey-combed, having been under water in the sea somewhere about fifty-five years—which will some day give them reason to repent their temerity. Before the day is spent, they all collect by order of the magistrate in front of the church, hoist the royal standard (which is a silk pocket handkerchief), and give three hearty cheers for their beloved Queen. Whenever an English man-of-war visits the island, the captain always inquires whether the magistrate has any complaint to make to him about any one on the island, or regarding the conduct of those belonging to any vessels which have called, since the last visit of a Queen's ship. Their laws, which relate chiefly to property, are enacted at public meetings.

"H. M. Sloop *Fly*, Callao, Jan. 25th, 1839.

"Sir,—After a long passage, I arrived at Pitcairn's Island on the 29th November, when I found this interesting community preserving their deservedly high character for exemplary morality, innocence, and integrity; but they very earnestly represented to me the immediate necessity for there being some chief, or head, to their increasing community (amounting now to ninty-nine souls), for their internal regulation and government; but more especially to meet the difficulties and dangers which they had already experienced, and were again threatened with, by lawless strangers in whale ships; there having been cases of recent occurrence, where half the ruffian crew of a whale ship were on shore for a fortnight, during which time, they offered every insult to the inhabitants, and threatened to violate any women whose protectors they could overcome by force, occasioning the necessary concentration of the men's strength for the personal protection of the females, and thereby great damage to their crops, which demanded their constant attention; taunting them that they had no laws, no country, no authority that *they* were to respect—American vessels denying that they were under the protection of Great Britain, as they had neither colours nor written authority. I found them, however, with a merchant union jack flying, procured from an English ship. Apprehending that my duty required some decided step in this unlooked for contingency, I considered I should best afford protection to these people, and least involve my own Government, of whose intention in respect to the Pitcairn islanders I am ignorant, by conferring the stamp of authority on their election of a magistrate or elder, to be periodically chosen from among themselves, and answerable for his proceedings to Her Majesty's Government, for whose information he is to keep a journal. I accordingly drew up a few hasty regulations, to be observed under my authority, in the election of this officer, marked No. 6.; which, with a formal attestation of his being sworn before me, and a union jack, which I supplied them with, will, I trust, insure them from any renewed insults from foreigners. By their unanimous voice, they selected for the situation Edward Quintal, a most able and superior senior of their number. I trust, sir, you will consider my assumption of the power to confer this authority, was warranted by the urgency of circumstances and the difficulty of reference; and that you will be able to approve of the view I have taken of my duty.

"I have the honour to be, Sir,
"Your very obedient servant,
" (Signed) R. ELLIOTT, *Commander.*

"To Rear Admiral C. B. H. Ross, C. B., &c., &c., &c."

By Russell Elliott, Esq., Commander of H. B. M. Sloop
Fly, and Senior Officer at Pitcairn's.

"REGULATIONS for the appointment of a magistrate at Pitcairn's, on the first day of January, every year. An elder or magistrate is to be elected by the free votes of every native born on the island, male or female, who shall have attained the age of eighteen years; or, of persons who have resided five years upon the island. And they shall assemble for such purpose in the schoolhouse the first day of every year, where the business shall be presided over by the magistrate of the preceding year, whose period of office does not expire until the swearing in of his successor. The greatest number of votes shall determine the election or re-election of the magistrate, whose duty it shall be to hold the chief authority on the island, and to settle all differences, with the advice of his council; which is to consist of two other natives, one to be named by the votes of the assembly, and the other by the magistrate himself; but his decision is final. It shall be the duty of the said magistrate, also, to keep a journal or register of all complaints made to him, and his decision on them; and if any grave offence, or serious crime, be committed, he is to secure the custody of the offender, until he has the opportunity of delivering him over to justice. He will submit his account of what has occurred to the captain of any British ship of war arriving; and hold himself responsible for the faithful and just fulfilment of the duties of his office. It will be incumbent on his countrymen, and the residents on the island, to respect his situation, and obey his authority, under pain of serious consequences, until he is superseded by the authority of Her Majesty the Queen of Great Britain. No one shall be eligible for the situation of magistrate, but a native-born inhabitant of the island. The following shall be the form of oath to be administered:—'I solemnly swear, that I will execute the duties of magistrate and chief ruler of Pitcairn's Island, to which I am this day called on the election of the inhabitants, by dispensing justice and settling any differences that may arise, zealously, fearlessly, and impartially; and that I will keep a register of my proceedings, and hold myself accountable for the due exercise of my office to Her Majesty the Queen of Great Britain, or her Representatives. So help me God.'

"Dated on board Her Majesty's Sloop *Fly,*
" off Pitcairn's Island, this thirtieth day of
" November, 1838.

"(Signed)   R. Elliott, *Commander.*"

" No. 1.—*Laws and Regulations of Pitcairn's Island.*

" The magistrate, is to convene the public on occasions of complaints being made to him; and, on hearing both sides of the question, commit it to a jury. He is to see all fines levied, and all public works executed; and every one must treat him with respect. He is not to assume any power or authority on his own responsibility, or without the consent of the majority of the people. A public journal shall be kept by the magistrate, and shall from time to time be read; so that no one shall plead ignorance of the law for any crime he may commit. This journal shall be submitted to the inspection of those captains of British men-of-war, which occasionally touch at the island.

"No. 2.—*Laws for Dogs.*

" If any one's dog is found chasing a goat, the owner of that dog shall pay a fine of one dollar and a half; one dollar to the owner of the goat or goats, and the other half to the informer. If a dog kills, or otherwise injures a goat, the owner of the dog so offending must pay the damage; but should suspicion rest on no particular dog, the owners of dogs generally must pay the damage. The foregoing law is of no effect when the goat or goats are upon cultivated ground. Persons who have fowls or hogs in the bush may take dogs to hunt them; but should the dogs commit damage during the hunt, the person taking the dogs to hunt must pay the damage.

"No. 3.—*Laws for Cats.*

" If any person under the age of ten years shall kill a cat, he or she shall receive corporal punishment. If any one, between the ages of ten and fifteen, kill a cat, he or she shall pay a fine of twenty-five dollars; half the fine to be given to the informer, the other half to the public. All masters of families convicted of killing a cat shall be fined fifty dollars; half the fine to be given to the informer, the other half to the public.

"N.B. Every person, from the age of fifteen and upwards, shall pay a fine similar to masters of families.

"No. 4.—*Laws for Hogs.*

"If a pig does any damage, the person who sustains the damage may take the pig so trespassing, no matter whether he see the pig committing damage, or another person see the pig committing damage. If any person or persons, see a pig, or pigs, committing damage, and neglect to inform the person sustaining the damage, the person guilty of such neglect must pay the damage.

"No. 5.—*Laws regarding the School.*

"There must be a school kept, to which all parents shall be obliged to send their children, who must previously be able to repeat the alphabet, and be of the age of from six to sixteen. Mr. Nobbs shall be placed at the head of the school, assisted by such persons as shall be named by the chief magistrate. The school-hours shall be from seven o'clock in the morning until noon, on all days, excepting Saturdays and Sundays, casualties and sickness excepted. One shilling, or an equivalent as marked below, shall be paid for each child per month, by the parents, whether the child attend school or not. In case Mr. Nobbs does not attend, the assistant appointed by the chief magistrate shall receive the salary in proportion to the time Mr. Nobbs is away.

"Equivalent for money:—

		s.	*d.*
One Barrel of Yams,	valued at -	8	0
One Barrel of Sweet Potatoes,	,, -	8	0

	s.	d.
One Barrel of Irish Potatoes, valued at	12	0
Three good Bunches of Plantains, ,,	4	0
One Day's Labour, ,,	2	0

"The chief magistrate is to see the labour well performed; and goods which may be given for money, shall be delivered, either at the market-place, or at the house of Mr. Nobbs, as he may direct.

"No. 6.—*Miscellaneous.*

"If any person wants to cultivate any lands, he is to give notice of it to the public; and any person wanting any wood is to go on the aforesaid land and get it. If any person cuts more wood than is sufficient to build his house, the wood that remains after his house is finished is to be given to the next person who may want it to build a house. This extends only to the mero and borou timber. Any person who may want any trees to break off the wind from his plantations or houses, is to make it known; and no one is allowed to cut them down, even if they be upon his own land. At any meeting which may take place, there shall be no bringing up things that are past to criminate others, with a view to prevent justice with the case before the magistrate. Any one doing so shall be punished by such a fine as a jury may think proper to award. The magistrate is to appoint churchwardens, four in number, beginning on the first of every month. Any person detected in shooting, or in any way killing white birds (unless it be for the sick), shall, for each bird that is killed, pay a dollar.

"No. 7.—*Laws for Wood.*

" If any person goes to cut logs, to enclose a piece of ground, or any other purpose, he is not to cut any fit for building a dwelling-house. The magistrate is to appoint four men to inspect the logs after they are brought home; and should any be found serviceable for building dwelling-houses, they are to be taken from him and given to the next person who builds a house. The third year from the time a person commences cutting wood for his house, he is to build it, and the second year he is to pick a share of thatch for covering dwelling-houses. If the wood is left longer than the time specified, it is to be taken from him and given to the next person who builds a house. Any person cutting logs, must not cut green ones until no more dry ones can be found. Any person without a pig-sty and wanting one, is allowed to cut green logs to make it with, if dry logs are not be found. No one is allowed to cut down any trees for logs on which there are young ones growing, which may become serviceable for building in future. Any person having a large enclosure round his pig-sty, cutting down any tree on which there is any good logs, is not allowed to take the logs, but he has to leave it for the benefit of those who have no enclosure. He is also bound to inform those who have no enclosure where the logs are to be found; but if they do not cut them at the end of two weeks, any one may be allowed to cut them, and keep them for such service as they please. No one may cut green logs to repair his large enclosure, save what he may find on trees which have been cut and left above two weeks.

"No. 8.—*Laws respecting Landmarks.*

"On the first day of January, after the magistrate is elected, he shall assemble all those who should be deemed necessary; and with them he is to visit all landmarks that are upon the island, and replace those that are lost. Should anything occur to prevent its accomplishment in the time specified (the 1st of January), the magistrate is bound to see it done the first opportunity.

"No. 9.—*Laws for Trading with Ships.*

"No person or persons shall be allowed to get spirits of any sort from any vessel, or sell it to strangers or any person upon the island. Any one found guilty of so doing shall be punished by fine, or such other punishment as a jury shall determine on. No intoxicating liquor whatever shall be allowed to be taken on shore, unless it be for medical purposes. Any person found guilty of transgressing this law, shall be severely punished by a jury. No females are allowed to go on board of a foreign vessel, of any size or description, without the permission of the magistrate; and in case the magistrate does not go on board himself, he is to appoint four men to look after the females.

"No. 10.—*Law for the Public Anvil, &c.*

"Any person taking the public anvil and public

sledge-hammer from the blacksmith's shop, is to take it back after he has done with it; and in case the anvil and sledge-hammer should get lost by his neglecting to take it back, he is to get another anvil and sledge-hammer, and pay a fine of four shillings."

Such as their code is, I give it word for word, although it will not be found very amusing; and the following, which have not been copied into the code, although in use upon the island:—

"If a fowl be seen trespassing in a garden, the proprietor of the garden is allowed to shoot and keep it, while the owner of the fowl is obliged to return the charge of powder and shot expended in killing the bird. This is the law; but the practice is to send back the dead fowl, and drop the claim for ammunition. If a pig be seen trespassing, no one is allowed to give information excepting to the owner of the land, that he may not be baulked in whatever course he may think to adopt.

"Squid (a glutinous fish, in shape not unlike a starfish) is not allowed to be taken for food from off the rocks at the north end of the island, excepting by the owner of the rocks; but any one may take it for bait, when going fishing."

"Carving upon trees is forbidden." It seems that the lads and maidens used to amuse themselves with carving true love-knots, which are considered by the elders, who had written their own long ago, as a practice fraught with danger. The trees generally used for the above purposes were the large banana and plantain, which are as easily written upon as paper, especially upon their leaves.

Public Works.

The magistrate for the time being is obliged to superintend the execution of all public works, among which are ranked the building of houses, fresh thatching them—which is necessary every seven years—reparations and alterations of the church, roads, and water-tanks, three of which have been lately cut out of the solid rock, on the west side of the island, for the supply of vessels, &c. In these public works, one member of each family (excepting that of Mr. Nobbs) is obliged to assist. With regard to the school-house and schoolmaster's residence, they are kept in repair, and altered as required, by the parents of those children who attend; the labour contributed by each family being proportionate to the number of children it sends.

When a man marries, he takes his share of his father's land, which land is equally divided among his children. The wife takes her proportion from her own father's land, and joins it to her husband's land, so that the young couple come immediately into their landed property. It may appear strange that even the rocks upon the seashore should be shared out as private property, but they are of value for the collection of sea salt.

The Church.

Divine service is performed in the school-house, which is capable of containing about 200 people. Two services are performed on Sundays. After the second service, a Sunday-school is held. The Communion Service, Gospels, and Epistles are read only on the first Sunday in the month. In the three following weeks, the Litany is read. They are also questioned on the Catechism the first Sunday in the month, during the afternoon service. Mr. Nobbs, to whom they look up with great respect of which he is most fully deserving, acts as minister; although, unfortunately, not in holy orders, on which account he does not venture to administer the Eucharist. They are much in want of a church bell, that which they now use being too small and cracked; it is rung for school as well as for church, and also whenever a vessel is reported in sight. No work is performed on Sunday, not even if a vessel should call at the island for provisions on that day, unless she be in actual necessity of them. Forty pupils attend the Sunday-school. There are three burial-places, containing but few tomb-stones; most of these have the name of the deceased engraved upon them, on copper from out of the *Bounty*. Their funerals are always attended by every person upon the island, even if the deceased be only an infant. Mr. Nobbs holds a Bible-class, every Wednesday evening, in his own house. The women are not allowed to marry under the age of sixteen. Prayers are read night and morning, in every house; and a blessing asked always at meals.*

* In 1814, when H. M. S. *Britain* called here, Thursday October Christian and George Young went on board; and being invited by Sir Thomas Staines to go down below and take some refreshment, the interest and surprise of the officers

Before quitting the church, I must mention that, although Mr. Nobbs has been of the greatest service to these islanders, he is now getting old and infirm, and ought to be allowed to retire, and his place occupied by a minister, if possible in holy orders, and one who knows a little of medicine; and this ought to be carried into effect immediately, either by H. M. Government, or some laudable religious society.

The School.

School hours are from 7 A.M. to 2 P.M., excepting Saturday, which is a sort of holyday to collect provisions, &c., for Sunday. When a vessel calls at the island, there is a general holyday, as every one is employed in collecting refreshments, &c., &c., for her. They seldom go off to a whaling vessel in a boat—using a canoe generally; but when an English vessel appears in sight, a boat goes off to her as soon as she is within a reasonable distance of the settlement. Reading, writing, geography, mathematics, &c., &c., are taught. Every child must be able to repeat the alphabet, Lord's Prayer, and Belief, before he goes to school. There are now about fifty scholars, some of whom have made very great progress. The writing of some, in particular, was equal to that which might be met with in any merchant's office in London. Many of them attend school until

was not a little increased when, on having provisions set before them, Christian rose up, and placing his hands in a devotional posture, repeated in a pleasing and serious tone of voice:—"For what we are going to receive may the Lord make us truly thankful!"

they are married, and some even afterwards. School is a great delight to the young people; they appear to be anxious to learn everything which they think will be of any sevice at all to them. I have often been much surprised to find many of them make use of words and sentences of which I little thought they could have known the meaning. Mr. Nobbs is schoolmaster, and receives one shilling per month for each pupil, which is generally paid in food by their parents; but, should he think proper to hire the parents for his garden, either in taking up or putting in crops, they are obliged to attend his call, at the rate of two shillings per diem. Mr. Nobbs is also the medical man of the island, and those families which he attends during the year, generally make him a present of different articles of food. There is a piece of ground on the first ridge, near the landing-place, among a grove of cocoa-nut trees, which has been set out as a market-place. To this, on the arrival of any vessel, the provisions that she may require are brought—Mr. Nobbs taking an account of what each family contributes. As all are entitled to share alike in the benefit of trade, no one is suffered to bring more than his proportion of the gross quantity required. There is a small house upon the ground, where the different articles of trade from the vessel are deposited, in case of wet weather. As soon as the order of the vessel is made up, everything is then carried down to the landing-place, to high-water mark; it is then considered in the captain's charge, who either takes it off in his own boat, or gives the islanders compensation for the use of theirs. Their system of agriculture is as primitive as are their manners. Totally unversed in the mysteries of subsoil ploughing, and ignorant of the virtues of guano, all their field-work is performed with the hoe; by the use of which, however, and by not sparing their own labour, they contrive to raise abundant crops of food, previously mentioned. I observed many patches of the tobacco plant; but they do not well understand the art of curing the leaf. There is a common wooden sugar-mill upon the island, but of an inferior description. The largest quantity of sugar ever made at one time, has been six cwt. They prefer making molasses to sugar, as they can make it go much further in their food, more especially among their children. The cane does not grow very large, and is but little cultivated, on account of the immense number of rats upon the island, which do great damage amongst the canes. Fish are not very numerous; but whenever the weather is fine, they seldom lose the chance of going out to catch them. The largest are a sort of cod, some of which are very fine eating. There is the red snapper, and a few other smaller sorts; the latter are caught near the shore, in shallow water; but the former they fish for in 100 to 200 fathoms, about one and a half or two miles from shore. They make their own fishing-lines, which they much prefer to ours; their own not being so liable to twist in deep water, which is the case with our lines in deep water, our lines being laid up too tightly. They make their lines of sail-twine, and purchase it whenever they get the chance of doing so. Crawfish are numerous at certain seasons, which they procure by diving for them a few feet under water, alongside the rocks. There are but few eatable shell-fish. Their domestic animals are in reality a loss to them, the quantity of food they supply being so small compared to what they consume; a consideration of great importance, when they are, for the most part, obliged to be kept up and fed upon the produce of cultivated land. A few of the goats are allowed to run loose upon some parts of the island; the number which each family is allowed to keep at one time, being proportioned to the number of its members, but it must never exceed nine. Those which run loose are generally female goats; the males being kept up at home, and fed three or four times a day, until two years old, when they are killed, or sold to the shipping. The females are always brought home a few days before kidding, after which they are again turned out until the kids are from three to four months old, when they are again brought home and marked; when the female kids and their mother are again turned out, and the males kept at home. The goats generally remain near the place where they were first turned out, which is accordingly selected as far as possible from the settlement and plantations. Pigs are fed much in the same manner as the goats, which makes them very expensive to rear; what few they have, they do not care to sell, as they are ashamed to ask a remunerating price for what they have actually cost in labour and potatoes. Each family generally kills a large hog when the yam digging

commences, as they are then obliged to work very hard.
They eat animal food, generally speaking, very sparingly, except at this season. Mr. Nobbs informed me,
that by the time a large hog (300 lb. weight) was fit
to kill, at this season, it usually ate about thirty barrels
of potatoes, which, at 8s. a barrel, would be £12; it
need therefore be a matter of no surprise that they
cannot afford to sell them at a reasonable price. Fowls
are small, but are bred in large numbers, and with
few exceptions, at some distance from the settlement,
on account of the great destruction they make amongst
the gardens in the settlement; they also do much
mischief to the banana and plantain trees, into which
they fly and eat the fruit as soon as ripe; against this
there is no remedy. The large breed of fowl which is
now reared in New Zealand—the chittagong or jungle,
or, as most people there erroneously call them, the Malay
fowl—would be of great value to them, as they are too
heavy to fly aloft into the trees. Any vessel that may
call and have such kind on board, would confer a great
benefit upon the islanders by making a fair exchange.
Their rabbits will, I fear, some day be a great nuisance
to them, there being no hawk or other enemies to keep
them under when once they get out into the bush,
where they most assuredly will without much care be
taken to keep them in confinement, which at present
does not appear to be the case. The dwelling-houses are
from forty to fifty feet long, about thirteen feet high,
and fifteen feet wide. There is no glass upon the
island, except one small window, which came out of the

Bounty, and which is in Mr. Nobbs's house. The windows, more like the portholes of a ship, go all round the houses, and are closed in bad weather with sliding shutters. One end of the house, about ten feet long is portioned off, as the sleeping apartment for the head of the family and his wife. Sometimes the other end is likewise cut off; when this is the case, it is generally occupied by one of the married children and family, who often still reside with the old people for some time. The whole side of the house, opposite the door-way, is fitted up with sleeping-berths, raised about three feet from the ground, for the rest of the family, each bed-place having its own window fitted like those in front. No house has any fireplace in it; the thermometer ranging from 55° to 85°. Their cook-houses for preparing their food, are always detached from their dwellings. They follow the fashion of the other South Sea islanders, forming ovens with hot stones in the ground. There are but few saucepans; but they are used for many purposes, when they can be obtained. They sometimes use ovens similar to our own, but very seldom. These are made of large flat stones, which are banked up with earth a foot wide, which earth is encased by another outside square of similar stones, so that the heat is most effectually kept in. Their food is chiefly fruit and vegetables; fish when they can procure it, and sometimes goats, which they shoot in the mountains. They are cleanly in their cooking, and take much trouble over it. They are very ingenious cabinet-makers, making neat workboxes and

dressing-cases, of a reddish streaked wood, the same as
that with which they build their houses, very handsome,
and rather lighter then rosewood in colour; many of
them being inlaid with a yellowish wood, which gives
them a handsome appearance, they sell readily for 20*s.*
to 30*s.* each, to parties who visit the island. They also
make very handsome walking-canes of the same wood,
as well as of the cocoa-nut and palm trees. The women
make hats and baskets from the leaves of this same
palm (the Pandanus), which leaves are likewise used in
thatching their houses. They sell as many of all the
above as they can make, every person coming on
shore wishing to carry away some memorial from this
interesting island. The population of the island is,
males, seventy-seven; females, seventy-nine; making
a total of one hundred and fifty-six. There are twenty
married couple; fifteen males unmarried, between the
ages of sixteen and twenty-five, and eleven females
between the same ages; one widow, Susannah, a Tahitian, who came in the *Bounty* (Young's widow, who
cut off the Tahitian's head, Tetihito, when he was
asleep). There is only one instance of twins, one of
whom I saw married. The great drawback to the
women not marrying more than they do, is chiefly on
account of the extra work which falls upon them; and
also, as many of them told me, on account of there not
being enough land on the island to support their
families. Hard times, indeed! The women generally
wear a petticoat from the hip downwards, and over that
a loose gown, often with a handkerchief thrown loosely

over their shoulders. A wreath of flowers round the head denotes their being unmarried. Their hair is worn in bands, with what was, to my eye, an incomprehensible knot. The men always wear short trousers, the legs of which are cut off about six inches above the knee. A shirt, and a cap or hat, complete their costume. On Sunday the men and women are very particular about their dress, which particularity was even extended to ourselves, for they sent us white shirts (we generally wore coloured ones), requesting we would put them on to go to church in. Children generally run about until they are two years old, in a state of nature. The men are, generally speaking, well formed and muscular, standing rather above the usual height. The women are neither tall nor short, but inclined to be rather stout, with a fine skin; some of them very fair, while others are as dark as Spaniards. Both men and women have fine teeth, especially the latter. The children come very early to the use of their limbs. I have seen one of these little imps walking about at the age of ten months, and was assured that he had been able to walk two months previously. Quarrels and swearing are unknown amongst these islanders, who are as one large family bred up together; they are, in point of fact, all more or less related to each other, and look upon each other more as brothers and sisters than anything else. The children appear to be more nursed by their relations than by their mothers, which makes it often difficult to distinguish the married from the unmarried. Whenever any passenger, captain, or boat's crew remain on shore all night, each individual is received into a different house for the night—an excellent plan, as the stranger can then be closely watched (how sad that surveillance should be ever needed to keep them out of mischief!); while far more information is obtained from them, than if they were lodged in a body, in which case only one would be able to speak at a time, and the contributions of the rest to the common stock of knowledge would be lost. The islanders generally take it in turns to entertain strangers, it being looked upon as a privilege rather than a troublesome duty.

Miscellaneous.

High-water at full and change, three hours after the moon rises. Rise and fall, eight feet (so say the islanders). Water may be had in almost any quantity (say three thousand gallons a-day) from the tanks on the west side. The best way of getting it off is to anchor about half a mile off shore, exactly off the watering-place, when the wind is in any way from the eastward, in about twelve fathoms. The casks are taken on shore in rafts, and rolled up to the tanks over a surface of flat rock; it is possible to land there, but not to haul a boat up on shore. The remuneration for watering is from 30*s*. to 60*s*., according to the quantity. Wood may be had, in cases of necessity, at three dollars a boat-load; but the islanders would rather not part with it, they themselves requiring a large quantity to boil their salt with. The island appears to be covered with wood, but no timber scarcely exceeds two feet in diameter. The following is a list of the provisions that can be annually spared from the island, and their prices:—

200 to 300 barrels of sweet potatoes, at per barrel, 8s.
100 to 150 ,, Irish ditto ,, 12s.
100 to 120 ,, yams ,, 8s.
1500 to 2000 cocoa-nuts, at per hundred 8s.
300 to 400 bunches of plantains, 3 bunches for 4s.
50 dozen fowls, - - at per dozen 12s.
40,000 to 50,000 oranges, at per hundred 4s.
10,000 ditto, at per barrel 8s.
100 gallons of lime-juice, at per gallon 2s.

Water melons, pumpkins, and beans, in almost any quantities.
Yams come in, in September.
Potatoes nearly all the year round.
Oranges in March.
Cocoa-nuts all the year round.
Pumpkins in March.
Plantains and bananas all the year round.
Water melons, in November.

For these clothing and tools, as well as money, are always acceptable in exchange. A stout, common turning-lathe would be of great benefit to them. Two or three hives of bees, which might be easily sent from New Zealand, are also much wanted there; as well as vegetable and flower seeds, fruit-trees, and some rose-trees—the last they much wish for. A good breed of large fowls, in place of those light mischievous ones. China boar and sow. Books—not twopenny tracts, for they are at a discount, a large box of them being nailed up in store when I was there, while the Homilies of the Church of England hold an honourable place in the greater number of their little libraries (each family having one). The American whaling captains, I think, charge too much in dealing with these people; they should let them have what little trade they require at but little above cost price. They are striving to make a living, and not a fortune. Whilst on the other hand, the prices for refreshment on the island are fixed, whether the crops are abundant or not. The admiral of the South American station has orders to see that the island is visited once a year by a Queen's ship, generally bringing some trifling present of clothing and other necessaries, for which the islanders manifest much more gratitude than the value of the gift can be fairly said to deserve. Great is the rejoicing when a man-of-war arrives; the women go on board, which they do not venture with a merchantman. The men ask the captain's advice, should anything be needed with regard to their own internal government, and are generally guided by it. The arrival of men-of-war being for the most part *vid* Valparaiso, the gift of the Home Government is often accompanied by an additional contribution from the Rev. Wm. Armstrong (British chaplain), who, with Mr. Turnbull and Rev. Mr. Rowlandson, is most indefatigable in their behalf. So many colonial vessels are now calling at the island, which will not continue of long duration, on their way to California, that the real situation of these truly interesting people must soon become more publicly known; and I trust that the kind-hearted and liberal-hearted will, when an opportunity offers, bear in mind the most deserving community, I may say, any one ever chanced to see. It will be seen that, by the shipping-list in 1846, there were forty-eight vessels touched at Pitcairn's Island. But what was it in 1847?—there were seventeen, and in 1848, only nine ships. This is accounted for by the whaling vessels, by which the islanders obtained the most of their clothing and other necessaries, leaving the South Seas. Now, I wish most particularly to inform my readers, and the public generally, that such being the case, unless something is done for these worthy islanders, they will have to get clothing from some other source, or go back to their primitive tappa cloth, which would be a step backwards in civilisation. Their island, I have no doubt, will support many more than there are at present living on it; but the fast increase of population is now becoming such, that what they are able to grow they will require for themselves. Consequently, they will have none for export, which will be a double privation,—first, in having nothing to trade with the shipping for clothing; and secondly, on account of having nothing to sell to the shipping. Shipping will never call there; they will then be completely out of the world, excepting being now and then visited by a British man-of-war. I can only say that, as I expect to see them shortly, I shall be happy to receive anything for them, and lay it out in what I know they most require for their general good. All presents are sent to Mr. Nobbs, who divides them out equally among the different families. The following are medicines most required by them:—

Opium, laudanum, tartar emetic, antimonial powder, carbonate of ammonia, sulphate of zinc, sulphate of ether, sulphur, prussic acid, digitalis, Friar's balsam, quinine, gum, camphor, ipecacuanha, Davis's powders, jalap, blister salve, bitter aloes, asafœtida, sweet spirits of nitre, adhesive plaster. The public tooth-drawing instruments are much out of order at present.

I have now put together an account of these good people, unlike any that I have before seen or heard of, after not a few years' rambling, having been to nearly every part of the world except the Mediterranean,—as ample in detail as could be well expected from a residence of only sixteen days. I am confident, indeed, that but little more remains to be described; for not only was I most assiduous in inquiring, from the day of landing to that of departure, but I was likewise met with a corresponding readiness on the part of the islanders, to supply the information which I required. They were evidently pleased with the interest taken in their affairs, and having nothing to conceal or to be ashamed of, were able to speak to me without any reserve. The gathering of the materials was a labour of love, and the after arrangement of them has served to beguile many hours of a voyage which would otherwise have been insufferably tedious and inconvenient.

*A True Copy of the Pitcairn's Island Register, from
1790 to 1850.*

1790. Jan. 23rd, H. M. S. *Bounty* burned; in the same year Fasto, wife of John Williams, died, October; October Thursday Christian born.

1791 *to* 1792. Matthew Quintal, Daniel M'Coy, Elizabeth Mills, and Charles Christian born.

1793. Massacre of part of the mutineers (Christian, Mills, Brown, Williams, and Martin) by the Tahitians. The Tahiti men all killed, part by jealousy among themselves, and others by the remaining Englishmen. Mary Christian born.

1794. A great desire in many of the women to leave the island; a boat built on purpose to remove them, launched, and upset. Fortunately for them that she did so; for had she launched out upon the ocean, where could they have gone? or what could a few ignorant women have done by themselves, drifting upon the waves? They must ultimately have fallen a sacrifice to their folly.

August 16th, a grave was dug, and the bones of all the white men that had been murdered were buried.

Aug. 17th, the first boat built and launched.

Oct. 3rd, the celebration of the murder of the Tahitians was held at Quintal's house.

1794. Nov. 11th, a conspiracy of the women to kill all the white men when asleep in their beds was discovered; they were all seized, a disclosure ensued, and all were pardoned.

Nov. 30th, the women attacked the white men, but no one was hurt; they were once more pardoned, and threatened the next time with death.

1795. May 6th, the first two canoes for the purpose of catching fish were made. Saw a vessel close in with the island; mutineers much alarmed; vessel stood out to sea, Dec. 27th.

1797. Endeavoured to procure a quantity of meat for salting, and to make syrup from the ti-plant (*Dracæna terminalis*) and sugar-cane.

1798. April 20th, M'Coy distilled a bottle of ardent spirits from the ti-root; the copper kettle of the *Bounty* made into a still—frequent intoxication the consequence; M'Coy in particular, who had fits of delirium, in one of which he fastened a stone round his neck, threw himself off the rocks into the sea, and was drowned.

1799. Matthew Quintal, having threatened to take the life of Young and Adams, which failed, the consequence was, that Young and Adams considered their lives in danger, and thought they were justified in taking away his life, which they did with an axe. Between

1794 *and* 1799. Sarah M'Coy, *alias* Quintal, Dinah Adams, Polly Young, John Mills, Robert Young, George Young, William Young, Edward Young, Dolly Young, Jane Quintal, Arthur Quintal, J. James Young, and Rebecca Adams, were born. Quintal lost his wife by a fall from the cliff, while in search of birds' eggs.

1800. Edward Young (sen.) died of asthma; Edward Quintal, Catherine M'Coy, and Hannah Adams, born.

1804. June. George Adams born, the last child of the first generation.

1808. Charles Christian, son of T. O. Christian, born. Ship *Topaz* of Boston, Capt. Folger, arrived. Between this and the last date, Joseph Christian born; James Young died.

1810 *to* 1813. Fletcher Christian, Sarah Christian, Mary Christian, William M'Coy, and John Quintal, born.

1814. Sept. 17th. H. M. S. *Britain* and *Tagus* arrived. Matthew Quintal drowned from a canoe, while in a fit, between this date and 1813. Matthew Quintal, Daniel M'Coy, Edward Christian, and Polly Christian, born. John Mills killed by falling from the rocks.

1815 *to* 1816. Hugh M'Coy, Maria Christian, Arthur and Peggy Christian, born.

1817. William Quintal born. Arrived, ship *Sultan*

1817. of Boston, Capt. Reynolds. Jenny, a Tahitian woman, left here in the *Sultan.*

1818 *and* 1819. Charles Christian, Mary Christian, Matthew M'Coy, and Kitty Quintal born.

1820. John Quintal and Thursday O. Christian born.

1822. Margaret Christian, Frederick Young, Martha Quintal, J. Charles Quintal, and Jane M'Coy born.

1823. Simon Young and Mahew born this year; the latter died.

Dec. 10th. Arrived, ship *Cyrus,* of London, Captain Hall; and John Buffett came on shore as schoolmaster, and John Evans also came on shore.

1824. Feb. 10th. John Buffett married.

April 25th. Phœbe Quintal, daughter of Arthur and Catherine Quintal, born.

July 23rd. Sarah, daughter of Daniel and Sarah M'Coy, born.

Oct. 3rd. Edward, the son of Edward and Dinah Quintal, born.

Nov. 26th. Dinah, daughter of George and Hannah Young, born. John Evans married Rachael Adams.

1825. Thomas Buffett, son of John and Dolly Buffett, born.

Jan. 28th. Polly Young born.

April 26th. Isaac Christian born.

July 9th. James Quintal born.

Dec. 5th. Arrived, H. M. S. *Blossoms,* Capt.

AND THE ISLANDERS. 111

1825. F. W. Beechy. During her stay, John Adams married.
1826. May 7th. Sarah, wife of Charles Christian died, aged 37.
 July 21st. John Buffett born.
 Sept. 8th. Betsy Young born.
 Oct. 23rd. Samuel M'Coy born.
 Dec. 19th. Jane Quintal left the island in the *Lovely*, of London, Capt. Blythe.
1827. Jan. 31st. Abraham B., son of Edward and Dinah Quintal, born.
 April 1st. George Adams married Polly Young.
 July 21st. Caroline Quintal born.
 Nov. 10th. John Adams born.
 Dec. 4th. W. M. Young born.
1828. May 27th. David Buffett born.
 Oct. 1st. Mary B. Christian born. Jemima Young born.
 Nov. 12th. Albina M'Coy born.
  „ 15th. George Nobbs came on shore to reside.
1829. Jan. 3rd. Jonathan Adams born.
  „ 12th. John M. V. Evans born.

 March 5th. | JOHN ADAMS DIED, AGED 65.

  „ 7th. Louisa Quintal born.
 April 14th. Mary, wife of John Adams, died.
 May 8th. Ruth Quintal born.
 Aug. 30th. Mirriam Young born.

1829. Sept. 30th. Moses Young born.
   Oct. 18th. Charles Christian married Maria Christian, Daniel M'Coy married Peggy Christian, and George Nobbs married Sarah Christian.
1830. Jan. 19th. Martha Young born.
   March 15th. Arrived, H. M. S. *Seringapatam*, Capt. Hon. W. M. Waldegrave, with a present of clothing and agricultural implements and tools from the British Government.
   „ 20th. R. P. Buffett born.
   April 7th. Rebecca Christian born.
   June 19th. Isaac Adams born.
   Aug. 3rd. W. Evans born.
   „ 18th. Philip M'Coy born.
   Sept. 19th. Reuben E. Nobbs born.
1831. Feb. 28th. Arrived H. M. Sloop *Comet*, Alexander A. Sandilands; and barque *Lucy Anne* of Sydney, Government vessel, J. Currey, master, for the purpose of removing the inhabitants of Pitcairn's Island to Tahiti.
   March 6th. All the inhabitants of Pitcairn's Island embarked on board the above named vessel, and sailed for Tahiti.
   „ 21st. Arrived at Tahiti; on the passage, Lucy Anne Quintal was born. Soon after our arrival at Tahiti, the Pictairn people were taken sick.
   April 21st. Thursday O. Christian died.
   „ 24th. John Buffett and family, Robert

1831. Young, Joseph Christian, Edward Christian, Charles Christian (3rd), Matthew Quintal and Frederick Young, sailed from Tahiti in a small schooner; but, owing to contrary winds, the aforesaid persons landed at Lord Hood's Island, and the schooner returned to Tahiti.

April 25th. Lucy Anne Quintal died.
,, 29th. Prudence, a native of Tahiti, died.
May 4th. George Young died.
,, 15th. Kitty Quintal (2nd), died.
,, 16th. Polly Christian died.
June 3rd. Edward Christian died at Lord Hood's Island.
,, 4th. Jane M'Coy died.
,, 6th. Nancy Quintal born.
,, 8th. Kitty Quintal (1st) died.
,, 9th. Nancy, a native of Tahiti, died.
,, 21st. John Buffett and the others on Lord Hood's Island embarked in the French brig *Bordeaux Packet,* and on the 27th landed upon Pitcairn's island. During our absence, our hogs have gone wild, and destroyed our crops. After we returned, we employed ourselves in destroying the hogs.
,, 25th. Charles Christian (2nd) died.
,, 27th. Daniel M'Coy (2nd) and Hugh M'Coy died.
Aug. 7th. Sun eclipsed.
,, 12th. Charles D. Christian born.

1831. Aug. 18th. Robert Young died at Pitcairn's island.

Sept. 2nd. American brig, *Charles Dagget*, of Salem, with the remainder of the Pitcairn people from Tahiti, arrived.

Nov. 6th. Edward Young died.

" 24th. Joseph Christian died.

1832. May 30th. Benjamin C. Christian born.

Aug. 30th. Esther Nobbs born.

Sept. 15th. Daniel M'Coy died.

" 16th. Dorcas and Lydia Young (twins), born.

Dec. 26th. Daniel M'Coy, sen., died.

" 28th. M'Coy, jun., born.

1833. Jan. 17th. John Quintal married to Maria Christian. Fletcher Christian married to Peggy Young M'Coy. Mary Evans born.

June 10th. Eliza Quintal born.

Sept. 1st. Fletcher C. Nobbs born.

" 24th. Jacob Christian born. Sarah M'Coy died.

Nov. 5th. Susan Quintal born.

1835. April 5th. Sarah Quintal born.

May 3rd. Arthur Quintal married Mary Christian.

Sept. 7th. Frances M. Nobbs born.

Nov. 27th. Edward Buffett born.

Dec. 23rd. George F. M. Evans born.

1836. Jan. 17th. Henry. J. Quintal born.

June 17th. Absolem Quintal born.

1836. Oct. 6th. Jane A. Nobbs born.
,, 30th. Charles Christian married Charlotte Quintal; Matthew M'Coy married Margaret Christian.
Nov. 10th. Polly Christian born.
1837. Feb. 4th. Ellen Quintal born.
June 19th. Robert Young born.
July 10th. Jane M'Coy born.
Aug. 6th. Daniel Evans born. Caleb Quintal born.
Oct. 22nd. Arthur Quintal married Martha Quintal.
Nov. 5th. John Quintal married Dinah Young.
,, 7th. Nathaniel Quintal born.
,, 18th. Robert Young died.
Dec. 16th. Andrew Christian born and died.
1838. June 13th. Maria L. Christian born.
July 4th. Ann M. Nobbs born.
,, 31st. Edward J. Quintal born.
Aug. 11th. Dinah M'Coy born.
Nov. 5th. John Quintal received a dangerous wound, by falling from a rock, while catching a goat.
,, 14th. Maria Quintal born.
,, 24th. John Quintal died, aged twenty-seven, of lock-jaw, in consequence of a wound in the foot.
,, 29th. Arrived H. M. S. *Fly*, Captain Russel Elliott, with a present from Rev. Mr. Rowlandson and congregation at Valparaiso. Capt. Elliott proposed electing a chief magistrate,

1838. which was adopted, and Edward Quintal was chosen, and sworn in.

This island was taken possession of by Capt. Elliot, on behalf of the Crown of Great Britain, on the 29th of November.

Dec. 23rd. John Quintal born.

1839. Jan. 2nd. Edward Quintal re-elected chief magistrate. Fletcher Christian and William Quintal elected councillors.

Feb. 6th. William Young died, aged forty.

March 24th. Thursday O. Christian married Polly Young.

July 5th. Joseph Quintal born.

„ 12th. Martha Evans born.

Sept. 1st. Edward J. Quintal died of croup.

„ 22nd. James Wingate J. Nobbs born.

Nov. 3rd. Catherine Christian born.

„ 9th. Arrived H. M. S. *Sparrow-hawk,* Capt. J. Shepherd, at 11 A. M. The captain, several officers, and General Friere, ex-president of Chili, landed. In the afternoon the school children were examined, and received the approbation of our respected visitors. Capt. Shepherd afterwards divided some valuable presents amongst them.

„ 10th. Capt. Shepherd and his officers attended Divine service twice. At 5 P.M. they went on board.

1839. Nov. 11th. Capt. Shepherd returned on shore, and several cases were submitted to him for decision.

,, 12th. In the afternoon all the inhabitants were assembled in the school-house, and Capt. Shepherd addressed them on various subjects connected with their welfare. He then distributed rewards among the children of the school, according to their respective merits. In the evening H. M. S. *Sparrow-hawk* sailed.

Dec. 3rd. M'Coy born, but soon died.

,, 4th. The above-named infant interred.

,, 7th. Joseph Napoleon Quintal born.

,, 13th. Isabella Emily Christian born.

,, 30th. L. Victoria Rose Quintal born.

Summary.

52 scholars attend the public school. 106 inhabitants : 53 males, 53 females.

1840. Jan. 1st. Arthur Quintal, sen., re-elected magistrate. George Adams and Arthur Quintal, jun., elected councillors.

,, 19th. A Sunday-school commenced.

Feb. 8th. Mrs. Nobbs received a severe contusion on the shoulder by the falling of a cocoa-nut from the tree.

,, 13th. Moses Young fell from a cocoa-nut tree, at least forty feet high, and was but slightly injured.

1840. April 18th & 19th. Experienced a severe gale from N.N.W., which did considerable damage to the breadfruit plantations and orange-trees. Considerable fears were entertained by some of the islanders for the safety of their houses; but, through the mercy of Him who "rideth upon the storm," no accident occurred. At daylight the gale broke. In consequence of the ill health of the teacher, no school was kept for some time. Mr. Buffett officiated on Sundays.

May 2nd. A serious altercation took place between Edward Quintal, sen., and John Evans, sen. The latter received several bruises on his head, back, and throat, and several scratches on the throat.

„ 10th. Harriet Augusta Quintal baptized.

June 7th. Wm. Quintal married to Maria Quintal, widow.

July 23rd. Julia Christian born.

Nov. 9th. Arrived the missionary packet, *Camden*, Capt. Morgan. Several of the boats went on board. 9 A.M. the captain landed, along with the Rev. Mr. Heath of the London Missionary Society, who brought with him several valuable presents from the Governor of New South Wales, from the Lord Bishop, and the Rev. Dr. Ross. In the afternoon Mr. Heath preached a most impressive sermon, which was listened to with much breathless attention. May the effect which it then produced be abiding! Capt.

1840. Morgan then addressed the congregation on that most important subject—the care of the soul. In the evening several persons met at Mr. Nobbs's house for religious conversation. Mr. Heath presided.

Nov. 10th. Early this morning the school was visited by Messrs. Heath and Morgan, and the scholars, individually and collectively, examined. The result was very satisfactory, and both teacher and pupils commended. At noon another exhortation was given by Mr. Heath. In the evening our friends went on board, and the *Camden* sailed for the Marquesas Islands, carrying with them our best wishes.

Dec. 13th. Margaret M'Coy confined, but the child soon died. 51 scholars attended school. 58, the Sunday-school. Number of inhabitants: 53 males, 55 females. 17 males and 16 females eligible to vote at the magisterial election.

1841. Jan. 1st. Arthur Quintal, sen., elected magistrate. Fletcher Christian and Arthur Quintal, jun., councillors. John Quintal born.

June 17th. Andrew Christian born.

Aug. 18th. Arrived H. M. S. *Curaçoa*, Capt. Jenkin Jones, twenty-one days from Callao; and a most opportune arrival it was, for there were at least twenty cases of influenza among us. Immediately after arriving at the settlement, Capt. Jones, with the surgeon of the

1841. ship (Dr. Gunn), visited the sick. Fortunately there had been a small medicine-chest fitted up for this island on board the ship, and there being also one on shore, the surgeon was able to prescribe freely and beneficially.

Aug. 19th. Capt. Jones met as many of the inhabitants at the school-house as were able to attend, and addressed them upon several subjects connected with their welfare; after which he read a letter to them from Admiral Ross, and caused a variety of very useful articles, the gifts of the Admiral, Capt. Jones, and Mr. Miller of Valparaiso, for general distribution, to be distributed among them in the school-house. Captain Jones then went on board, and most humanely allowed Dr. Gunn to remain on shore all night.

„ 20th. The surgeon of the *Curaçoa* has been most indefatigable in his attention to the sick; and the result is, that many are beginning to mend, and all have experienced relief. There is not one resident upon the island who is not under weighty obligations to Dr. Gunn. At 4 P.M. the *Curaçoa* sailed. May Almighty God preserve the worthy captain, officers, and crew, from every untoward circumstance!

„ 31st. The number of sick began to increase. There are more than fifty cases. There is not a sufficient number of persons to dig the yams, this being the harvest season. Edward Quintal

1841. is not expected to survive many days, neither is his wife. The school-house is shut up, and nearly every house is like a hospital. Truly the hand of God is upon us. O Lord, in wrath remember mercy!

Sept. 5th. Sunday, but one service. This day the number of sick increase, although there are few convalescent. The epidemic is fever, attended with a distressing cough.

„ 8th. Edward Quintal, sen., died. His disease was influenza and dysentery combined. Three fresh cases of influenza.

„ 9th. Just in the height of preparing for the funeral of the deceased, a ship was reported, and shortly after the boat landed; it proved to be the ship *Mechanic*, of Rhode Island, Capt. Wates. Peggy Christian confined with a male child.

„ 10th. The woman delivered yesterday is attacked with dysentery.

„ 19th. Died, Isabella, a native of Tahiti, relict of Fletcher Christian of the *Bounty*. Her age was not known; but she frequently said she remembered Capt. Cook arriving at Tahiti. Some individuals are much better; others are in a precarious state.

„ 26th. Stephen Christian baptized.

„ 28th. School recommenced.

Oct. 2nd. Joseph Napoleon Quintal died, aged two years.

1841. Oct. 6th. Agnes Christian born.
„ 11th. Mary M'Coy born.
„ 17th. Matilda Quintal born.

Summary.

Births this year, 7; deaths, 3; marriages, 0. During the latter part of the year, the inhabitants have been much afflicted with bodily sickness. Ships holding communication with the island 19, and 1 passed. Inhabitants: males, 54; females, 57. 21 males and 17 females eligible to vote at the magisterial election. 50 scholars attend the Sunday-school.

1842. Jan. 2nd. Fletcher Christian, sen., elected magistrate. William Quintal and Matthew M'Coy, councillors.
„ 14th. Charles Christian, sen., died, after a lingering illness.
„ 22nd. Rhoda Quintal born.
Oct. 5th. George Adams fell from a tree, by which he was much injured.
„ 10th. Oliver M. Quintal born.
Dec. 3rd. A sad accident this day befel Stephen Christian, an infant fifteen months old. During the temporary absence of its mother, the child overturned an iron pot of hot water, by which it was dreadfully scalded.
„ 8th. Adeline Sophia Christian born.
„ 10th. Stephen Christian died, in consequence of his accident on the 3rd.

Summary.

1842. Births this year, 3; deaths, 2. Several cases of inflammatory fever exist at present. Ships holding communication with the island, 31. Inhabitants: males, 53; females, 59. 20 males and 20 females eligible to vote at the magisterial election. 50 children attend Sunday-school.

1843. Jan. 2nd. Matthew M‘Coy elected magistrate; Arthur Quintal and Simon Young, councillors.

„ 7th. Two persons yesterday, and three this day, have been attacked with the fever, which is of an inflammatory type, commencing with a shivering, succeeded by violent pain in the loins and head, and much febrile heat. Emetics and application of warm water to the feet, hands, and loins, are the principal remedies applied; and under the Divine blessing, they have been attended with beneficial results.

March 4th. Eleven of the inhabitants sailed in the barque *America*, for the purpose of exploring Elizabeth Island.

„ 5th. Arrived H. M. S. *Talbot*, Capt. Sir T. Thompson, Bart.; after remaining on shore, and adjusting some of the most pressing judicial cases presented to him, Sir Thomas went on board, and sailed for Valparaiso.

„ 11th. Barque *America* returned from Elizabeth Island, our people bringing a very unfavourable report of it.

1843. March 31st. Albert Christian born.
April 16th. John Adams married to Caroline Quintal. Mary Quintal born.
„ 23rd. Mary Quintal, wife of Arthur Quintal, died, aged 24.
May 5th. George E. C. Nobbs born.
„ 21st. Regia Quintal born.
Oct. 5th. Stephen Christian born.
Nov. 16th. Mary M'Coy born.
Dec. 17th. Polly Adams died from cancer in the breast.

Summary.

Number of births this year, 6; deaths, 2; marriage, 1. Much sickness experienced. Ships touched here, 29. Inhabitants: males, 59; females, 60. 20 males and 21 females eligible to vote. The public school has been closed since August, from the illness of the teacher.

1844. Jan. 8th. Thursday O. Christian elected magistrate. John and William Quintal elected councillors.
May 16th. Polly Young born
June 2nd. Edward Quintal born. Several cases of fever and cough, and oppression of the stomach, chiefly among young children.
July 31st. Isaac Christian married to Mirriam Young.
„ 28th. Arrived H. M. S. *Basilisk*, Capt. Henry Hunt, bringing presents to the inhabi-

1844. tants, from the British Government, Admiral Thomas, and from the Rev. Mr. Armstrong and other friends in Valparaiso.

July 29th. Capt. Hunt assembled the inhabitants, and disposed of such cases as were presented to him for adjudication.

,, 30th. The presents above mentioned were landed. The surgeon, Dr. Johnson, vaccinated sixty of the inhabitants, and prescribed for several cases of sickness.

,, 31st. Capt. Hunt assembled the inhabitants, made some alterations, and suggested others, for the improvement of the community generally. Appointed a commercial agent, and in the evening sailed for the Sandwich Islands.

Aug. 1st. Re-opened the public school. Edward Quintal baptized. This child was born on July 8th.

,, 12th. All our hopes concerning the late vaccination are at an end; it has turned out a complete failure.

Sept. 9th. Gilbert Christian born. The first fortnight was devoted to surveying and adjusting boundaries and landmarks, not having completed it, it is to be resumed after the yam planting is over.

Oct. 6th. George Adams, widower, and Sarah M'Coy, widow, married. Levi W. Quintal born on the 10th instant.

Summary.

1844. Births this year, 5; deaths, 0; marriages, 2. Ships touched here, 18. Inhabitants: males, 60; females, 61. 24 males and 28 females eligible for voting at the magisterial election. Weeds overrun the island. Worms infest the potatoes. There is a comet in sight. 44 children attend the school.

1845. Jan. 1st. Arthur Quintal, jun., elected magistrate. William M'Coy and Thomas Buffett, councillors.

,, 7th. Elias Christian born.

,, 19th. During the last week we have been employed in fishing up two of the *Bounty's* large guns. For fifty-five years they have been deposited at the bottom of the sea, on a bed of coral, guiltless of blood, during the time so many thousands of mankind became (in Europe) food for cannon. But on Saturday last one of these guns resumed its natural vocation—at least the innoxious portion of it—to wit, belching forth fire and smoke, and causing the island to reverberate with its bellowing; the other gun is condemned to silence, having been spiked by some one in the *Bounty*.

Feb. 15th. Ephraim Christian born.

March 13th. The fever has made its appearance amongst us; three of us have been attacked. It is of a bilious type.

,, 15th. The sick are better. No fresh cases.

1845. March 19th. Eight fresh cases this day. Violent pain in the head, burning heat, and cramp in the arms and thighs, are what the afflicted complain of chiefly; to which is added, in some cases, a dull pain in the back.

,, 21st. Fourteen more are on the list, and several others complaining. The teacher, who is also doctor, is continually on the run. Vomits and jalap are the order of the day. There is not a house but what there are one or more sick in.

,, 22nd. The numbers of the sick are greatly on the increase. Those first attacked are getting better, but more than thirty are on the list. The teacher is also sick, and it is with great difficulty he can get from house to house.

,, 23rd. Some of those first attacked have had a relapse; others seem quite well in health, but complain of great weariness. Seven fresh cases this day. The vomits in the medicine-chest nearly expended; more than sixty have been administered.

,, 24th. There is a ship in sight. A canoe has gone on board to ask for emetics. The canoe has returned with twelve doses of tartar emetic. The ship appearing was a providential circumstance. I will now say a few words about the salubrity of the island. It is generally supposed to be a healthy spot; indeed appearances seem to indicate such a conclusion; but

1845. the reverse is found, from experience, to be a fact. Asthma, rheumatism, consumption, scrofula, and, last but not least, influenza, under various modifications, are prevalent. Five times, within the last four years, has the fever been rife amongst us, though it has not been so severe lately. This, I think, may be accounted for by the teacher (doctor) becoming more acquainted with the nature of the disease (thanks to Dr. Gunn), and also with the appropriate remedies. When the influenza appeared among us at first, it did not spread so rapidly as it has done at its subsequent re-appearance; but the cough was more violent than it has been since. This I attribute to the teacher's not giving them emetics as soon as the disease attacked them. Since then, emetics have been immediately given on the disease appearing, which prevents any considerable degree of cough. But there is one particular in the recent fever that differs from the previous one; viz., in the total absence of the cold fit at the commencement. I have seen some of the patients, when first attacked, tremble as violently, and apparently from the same causes, as ever I saw any one who had a fit of the ague. In the last sickness it was not thus: one person complained of cold, and he was only slightly affected. The first man attacked was a man of full habit of body, plethoric, and subject to fits. He had attended Divine service in the morning—it being the Sabbath. After evening service, I found him under the influence of raging fever; his eyes seemed ready to start from their sockets, and the heat of his skin caused a disagreeable sensation to those who touched him. He complained of violent pains in his head, back, and thighs, and said he felt as if living things were creeping between his flesh and skin. Fearing it might bring on one of the fits to which he was subject, the teacher bled him, and gave him a soporific, which had a good effect. The next day a dose of calomel and jalap was given, and two days after he was well, but very weak. I do not think the fever was infectious; but though, in the space of six days, not less than sixty out of one hundred and twenty-two were attacked, yet I attribute it solely to the peculiar state of the atmosphere. Whenever we have been visited by this epidemic, the circumstances, as respect the weather, have been invariably the same. A long drought, succeeded by two or three weeks of rain, and the wind setting in from the north-west—in fact, a north-west wind is always the forerunner of rheumatism, catarrh, and slight febrile affections. Bleeding is not to be recommended; vomits are the sovereign remedy, for certainly no commu-

1845.   nity of persons secrete a greater quantity of
bile than the inhabitants of this island.

March 31st. There is now but one person sick, and
she is recovering. A few have a slight cough,
which is wearing away. And now it behoves
us to offer up our grateful thanksgiving to
Almighty God, Father, Son, and Holy Spirit,
to whom be glory, now and for ever, Amen.

April 16th. For several days past the weather has
been cloudy, with occasional showers. Wind
s.s.w.; it began to rain in good earnest. As
the day declined, the wind increased. At
sunset it blew a gale; all hands employed in
securing the roofs of their houses, and making all snug before dark. A dirty night was
anticipated, and our fears were realized. At
ten o'clock the wind shifted four or five points
to the westward, and the sheet lightning
began to break the monotony of the lucid
atmosphere. By midnight a perfect typhoon
raged above and around us; the whole con-
cave of the heavens was in a continued blaze,
and the roar of the thunder, though not so
very loud, *with the exception of one burst*, was
incessant. From the position of the wind,
which veered and hauled four or five points,
the houses were a good deal sheltered from its
violence, or they would most assuredly have
been prostrated; therefore, the most of us,
who passed a sleepless night, were, in mercy,

1845.   permitted to remain quiet in our houses. Very frequently, through the night, loud crashes were heard, which we supposed were the trees in the higher parts of the island yielding to the fury of the storm. The noise did not proceed from the falling and crashing of trees, but from a cause of which we were at that time happily ignorant. At daylight a man, much alarmed, came to my house, saying a part of the island had given way, and was falling into the sea. From the door of my house I observed an imperfect view of the spot from which a portion of earth had been detached, and felt certain that it was an avalanche, occasioned by the wind acting upon the trees, and the torrents of rain which fell detaching the earth from the part above it. So great was the consternation and amazement of the natives, that, although they had seen the spot from which the earth had slipped every day of their lives, yet they could not so far collect their ideas as to remember the original appearance of the place, whose property it had been, nor the locality near it. . As to the cause of the disruption various opinions prevailed. Some said it was occasioned by a water-spout; others, that a thunder-bolt had fallen there; and a third party were anxiously inquiring if it were not probable the sea had perforated a hole from the underside, and washed it away. That they had considerable occasion for alarm cannot be disputed; and what may easily be referred to natural causes, and those not recondite either, would, to persons so inexperienced as our community, appear both mysterious and awful. I will endeavour to describe, in a few words, what presented itself to our view at daylight. Going out of our doors at daylight, we saw that a considerable portion of earth had been detached from the side of the hill, but to what extent we could not then ascertain. The place in question was situated at the head of a ravine, which debouched into the sea; the rain, mixing with the falling earth, which was of a clayish nature, brought it to the consistency of thick mud, but sufficiently liquidated to glide very slowly down the inclined plane of the valley. Nothing that came in contact with it could resist its force; the large trees at the head of the ravine, and immense pieces of rock, were borne slowly but unresistingly along, and about three hundred cocoa-nut trees were torn up by the roots, and carried into the sea. So tenacious was the heterogeneous stream, that some, being displaced from their original situation, remained in an upright position for some time, and when they fell, it was many yards from the spot from which they had come to maturity. A con-

1845. siderable portion of this aquatic lava (for indeed its appearance had a distant resemblance to the molten streams of an active volcano) had reached the sea before daylight, and when some of our people ventured to the edge of the precipice, they found, to their dismay, the boat-houses and boats left there had disappeared. Two families, whose houses were adjacent to the ravine, removed their household goods, fearing the foundation of their dwellings might become undermined, and bury them underneath; but, in a few hours, the stream ceased to flow, and confidence was in a measure restored. We had now time to turn our attention to other parts of the island. At Bounty Bay a great quantity of earth had been washed away; a yam ground, containing 1000 yams, totally disappeared; several fishing-boats destroyed; the *Bounty*'s guns washed to the edge of the surf; and large pieces of rock so encumbered the harbour, that if a ship should come, it is doubtful whether a passage could be found for her boat to pass through. In the interior, all the plantain patches were levelled, and about 4000 plantain trees destroyed—one half in full bearing, and the other half designed for the year 1846, so that this very valuable article of food we shall be without for a long time. The fact is, that from this date until August, we shall be

1845. pinched for food. But God tempers the wind to the shorn lamb; and we humbly trust that the late monitions of Providence, viz., drought, sickness, and storm, which severally have been inflicted upon us this year, may be sanctified to us, and be the means of bringing us one and all into a close communion with our God. May we remember the rod, and he who appointed it! may we flee to the cross of Christ for safety and succour in every time of need, always bearing in mind our Heavenly Father doth not willingly afflict the children of men!

May 13th. Jemima Sarah Nobbs born.
June 26th. Nathan Christian born.
Sept. 4th. James R. M'Coy born.
Oct. 12th. John Buffett and Betsy Young married. Henry Christian born.
Nov. 28th. Gilbert W. F. Adams born.

Summary.

Births this year, 7; deaths, 0; marriages, 2. Number of inhabitants: males, 65; females, 62. At present the island is in a healthy state. Twenty-two American, two French, and one Dutch vessel, have visited us this year. We are most anxious to see a ship. A rumour of war reached us two months ago, and we want to ascertain the truth of it. Hoping it may be an unfounded report, we humbly beseech the Almighty to watch over

1845. our fatherland; and whether enjoying peace or engaged in war, may it never succumb to insult nor advocate oppression! 51 children attend the school. The people are busily employed preparing timber for enlarging our church.

1846. Jan. 1st. Arthur Quintal re-elected magistrate. William M'Coy and Thomas Buffett re-elected councillors.
,, 27th. Frederick L. F. Young born.
May 27th. Abbey L. T. Quintal born.
June 12th. Church and school-house finished. It is a very decent building, and reflects much credit upon the persons employed in the construction of it.
,, 14th. Opened the new house for public worship. Sermon for the occasion, 31st chap. Deuteronomy, 12th verse.
July 19th. Eleanor C. Quintal born.
Aug. 3rd. Alphonzo D. Christian born.
,, 29th. This morning Levi Quintal, an infant under two years of age, went into the cook-house, during the absence of his mother, and his clothes catching fire, he was burned in a dreadful manner. The next day the little sufferer died.
Sept. 14th. Sickness is again making a sad inroad among us. Fever, succeeded by dysentery, is the type. Some are afflicted severely, others

1846. slightly. Susannah, who came here in the *Bounty,* fifty-seven years ago, is in a dangerous state.

Sept. 18th. Emma Young born.

Nov. 11th. Edward J. N. Quintal born.

„ 27th. Alfred A. Nobbs born.

Summary.

Births this year, 7; marriages, 0; death, 1. Inhabitants: males, 69; females, 65. Sickness has been rife among us—fever, dysentery, and ophthalmia. Ships called here: American, 46; French, 1; Bremen, 1; English, 1:—49. 47 children attend public school.

1847. Jan. 5th, Charles Christian, sen., elected magistrate. Simon Young and John Adams, councillors.

Feb. 20th. This afternoon, as Reuben Nobbs was out in the mountain, shooting goats, his foot slipped, and he let fall his musket, which exploded and wounded him severely. The ball entered a little below the hip-joint, and passing downwards, came through on the inside of the thigh, about half-way between the groin and the knee. Providentially some persons were within call, who immediately ran to his assistance, and tore up their shirts to stanch the blood, which was pouring forth profusely. A lad was despatched to the vil-

1847. lage with the melancholy news, and in a few minutes, the whole of the inhabitants capable of going were on their way to afford relief, headed by his affectionate mother, who was almost frantic with grief. In about an hour they returned, bearing him in a canoe, which they had taken up for that purpose. After some difficulty the blood was stanched, and the lad suffered but little pain. Every person was anxious to render some assistance; the greater part of the male inhabitants remained at night, to be ready at a moment's warning to do anything that might be required. Towards midnight he fell asleep,—and so ends this melancholy day.

Feb. 21st. About daylight the wounded lad awoke, very much refreshed; he does not complain much, and has but little fever. The men and grown lads have formed themselves into three watches, to attend his wants both day and night. It is most gratifying to his parents to see the esteem in which their son is held.

„ 22nd. Reuben Nobbs is free from pain, but there is a considerable accession of fever; it does not appear that either the thigh or hip bone is injured, as he can move his leg without much difficulty or pain. From the great length of the internal wound, it is difficult to ascertain whether any of the wadding

1847. remains where the ball must have passed through.

Feb. 26th. This morning a ship was reported; everybody appeared rejoiced, hoping to get some necessaries for their wounded friend. On her nearing the island, she proved to be H. M. S. *Spy*, Capt. Woodbridge. "Thank God!" was the grateful exclamation of many, on hearing it was a ship of war, on account of her having a surgeon on board. At one P.M., Capt. Woodbridge and the surgeon (Dr. Bowden) landed, who immediately visited young Nobbs, and after probing the wound, and ascertaining the extent of the injury, gave his opinion that there was not much danger, and that with proper attention he would in all probability recover, although a narrower escape from death never came beneath his notice. Capt. Woodbridge, being much pressed for time, informed the inhabitants he must sail that evening. After kindly interesting himself in the welfare of the island, and noting down such things as the community were most in want of, at sunset the *Spy* sailed for Valparaiso. Mr. and Mrs. Nobbs would here take the opportunity of publicly recording their grateful acknowledgments to Capt. Woodbridge and Dr. Bowden, for the favours conferred on their son.

1847. Feb. 28th. Emma Young much burned by falling into a fire.

March 7th. Emma Young recovering from her late accident.

,, 10th. Reuben Nobbs in a convalescent state, but complains of much pain in the hip.

May 3rd. Harriet Melissa M'Coy born.

,, 7th. Henry Seymour Buffett born.

,, 24th. William B. S. Christian born.

June 4th. Experienced a heavy gale from the westward, which, if it had been of long duration, would have done incalculable damage. A large piece of the banyan-tree was blown down, and the flag-staff broken into two pieces.

,, 5th. Matthew M'Coy narrowly escaped with his life, his canoe being upset in the surf, on the west side of the island, and broken to pieces, and himself very severely bruised; had it not been for the assistance of two other persons near at hand, he must (humanly speaking) have been drowned.

Oct. 1st. Byon S. M. Adams born.

Nov. 2nd. Eliza C. P. Young born.

Dec. 24th. Almira Emeline Christian born.

Summary.

Births this year, 6; deaths, 0; marriages, 0. Inhabitants: males, 72; females, 68. Ships visited the island, 19. 48 children attend the school.

1848. Jan. 1. George Adams elected magistrate. William Quintal and John Adams, councillors.

Feb. 4th. As William M'Coy was assisting to carry a heavy piece of timber, his foot struck a small pointed stick, which entered among the sinews of the third and fourth toes, and broke off considerably below the surface. Attempts were made to extricate it, but without success. Laudanum was injected into the wound, and a bread poultice applied. The next morning the teacher dilated the wound, as much as the patient would let him; the teacher being fearful of cutting deep, on account of the proximity of the tendons. For three days laudanum was injected, and meal poultices applied thrice a-day; each morning an attempt was made to extract the piece of wood, but the patient was so susceptible of pain, that he could hardly permit the probing of the wound. The teacher being anxious that suppuration should take place, and knowing that laudanum would retard it, changed his practice, and substituted spirits of turpentine for laudanum, and basilicon for poultice. Things went on in this train several days, the patient suffering severe pain in his foot, his groin, and lower part of his belly. All attempts to extricate the wood were abortive. Serious fears were now entertained, which at last

1848. were fully verified. The teacher had been careful not to mention his suspicions to any one, lest they should reach the ears of the sufferer; but on the 13th, he was informed that M'Coy complained of a slight pain in the back of his neck, and that his jaws were somewhat stiff. Powerful anti-spasmodics were immediately applied, internally and externally, and repeated during the night, the teacher remaining with him; at daylight the sufferer was informed that death was inevitable, if the splinter were not extracted, when he consented to a further dilatation of the wound. The teacher too, urged by the desperation of the case, was determined to use more powerful means than he had hitherto done; accordingly the injured limb had a bandage bound tightly round it, and the patient being held down by several persons, a pair of plyers, reduced for the purpose, were inserted, and after many failures, the teacher succeeded in drawing forth a piece of wood three inches long, and half-an-inch in diameter. Laudanum was now injected into the hole, and continued to be so at intervals during that day and night; but the tension of the jaws and the stiffness of the neck continuing to increase, spirits of turpentine were again applied. Strong anti-spasmodics were administered, and friction with the hand upon

1848. the jaws and neck was untiringly and almost unceasingly applied; on the evening of the 15th, his jaws became fast closed, but in such a manner that he could imbibe small portions of liquid substances, and they frequently produced the symptoms of a person labouring under hydrophobia, he being now unable to swallow any preventive medicine. On the 17th, William M'Coy ceased to exist, aged thirty-eight. As a member of the community, William M'Coy's conduct was ever worthy of imitation; a dutiful son, a loving brother, and a firm friend. Being unmarried, he left no issue; his lands he bequeathed to his niece, Jane M'Coy, daughter of his brother, Matthew M'Coy.

Feb. 7th. Helen Amelia Quintal born.

March 9th. Arrived H. M. S. *Calypso*, Capt. H. J. Worth. From some misunderstanding respecting the signal, no attempt to land was made this day; our boat went on board and remained all night.

„ 10th. At 9 A.M. Capt. Worth and a party of officers landed, and the greeting on both sides was most cordial; our people—men, women, and children, are almost beside themselves. Two whale boats and several large cases of useful articles were landed for the use of the island, contributed by the Admiral and officers on the coast, and foreign residents in Valparaiso,

1848. among which, the Rev. Messrs. Armstrong (our untiring benefactor), and Turnbull were prominent. At 12 A.M. Capt. Worth and his officers returned on board to afford opportunity for another party visiting us. Much intreaty was used by our people to induce Capt. Worth to remain another day, and our young women drew up a petition and presented it to him. He did not give a decided answer about it; but told them that if they heard a gun in the night, it would be a signal for sailing. At 1 P.M. another party landed and returned on board at 4 P.M. Thus ends a very happy day; but much anxiety will be experienced during the night, lest the report of a gun should be heard. Fair weather, and fine weather, and light winds, is the earnest wish of all concerned.

March 11th. At daylight this morning, the general inquiry was, "Where is the ship?" She was discovered about four miles from the land. Two of our boats went on board, and at 9 A.M. the Captain landed. Dr. Domet, hearing there were hieroglyphics supposed to have been cut out by the aborigines on the face of the cliff, on the east side of the island, determined to inspect them himself. He was informed that the path was not only difficult but dangerous; yet he would not be turned from his purpose.

1848. Accordingly, he started with one of the islanders and succeeded in his undertaking, being the first European that ever went down the face of the cliff (which is very precipitous), without the assistance of a rope. At noon, Capt. Worth assembled the inhabitants, and expressed to them his entire satisfaction with the state of things on the shore, and exhorted them to continue in the way they were in. After making them presents of various articles from his own stores, he returned on board. The cutter soon returned with another party, and Lieut. M'Leod and Mr. Lock (midshipman) succeeded in descending the "ridge of the rope." At sunset, the cutter went on board, and the *Calypso* sailed, carrying with her our grateful aspirations that she may successfully accomplish the objects of her cruise, and return unscathed to Valparaiso. To Capt. Worth and his officers we are under weighty obligations, particularly to Lieut. M'Leod and Dr. Domet, though, in fact, every officer that came on shore seemed anxious to confer favours upon us. May God have them in his holy keeping, and may they long hold a place in our grateful recollections!

March 13th. Employed dividing the several articles brought hither in H. M. S. *Calypso*. The majority of the things were such as we

1848. were greatly in need of. Surely no community of people were ever so kindly cared for as we are.

March 30th. Cordelia R. Christian born.

April 9th. Jonathan Adams and Phœbe Quintal were married.

„ 29th. Wm. W. Quintal born.

May 27th. Sydney Herbert Nobbs born.

July 8th. Alice Sophia M'Coy born.

„ 9th. Moses Young and Albina M'Coy married.

„ 31st. Anna Rose Christian born.

Nov. 15th. George Colvin Clifton Adams born.

Dec. 25th. Abraham B. Quintal and Esther M. Nobbs were married.

Summary.

Births this year, 7 ; death, 1 ; marriages, 3. Inhabitants: males, 74 ; females, 72. Ships calling here, this year, 9. 44 children attend the school. 30 scholars, of 14 years of age and upwards, attend the Sunday-school. The attendance at the Wednesday Bible-class for adults quite satisfactory.

1849. Jan. 1st. Simon Young elected magistrate. Arthur Quintal and Edward Quintal, councillors.

„ 16th. Mary Edward Young born.

April 19th. George Webb Adams born.

March 24th. Rachael E. Young born.

July 10th. This morning, at daylight, our city

1849. was scared from its propriety by the booming of a cannon. Those who had already risen, ran to the edge of the precipice; and those who had not turned out, lost no time in doing so. A brig was discovered in the offing, with a flag of some kind flying; but from the want of light we could not distinguish its heraldic bearings. After peeping through the somewhat hazy atmosphere for nearly half an hour, and stretching our necks and eyelids in a most extraordinary manner, the increased light enabled us to discern that the vessel wore the St. George's ensign, and now the shout of "a man-of-war" sounded from house to house. Two boats were speedily manned, and soon got on board. As the weather was louring, we were fearful on shore that the ship's boat would not land; but after an hour's anxious surprise, we were gratified by seeing a boat lowered, and shortly after pull for the shore, accompanied by our boats. On nearing the surf, a party from the ship's boat shifted into ours and passed through the surf quite dry. The brigantine proved to be H. M. S. *Pandora*, Capt. Wood, from Oahu and Tahiti, bringing us Mr. Buffett back who left here for the Sandwich Islands, last January. Capt. Wood brought with him letters from Consul-General Miller and several other persons, offering to provide land,

1849. &c., &c., for any families who wish to emigrate from here and go there. Capt. Wood assembled the inhabitants at the schoolhouse; and on the letters being read, informed them that he would remain on shore till the afternoon of the next day, in order that they might have time to deliberate on the contents of the letters, and then he would receive their answers.

July 11th. This evening, Capt. Wood left us, to our great regret; for though our acquaintance was but of two days' duration, the urbanity of Capt. Wood and his solicitude for our welfare have made a deep, and we hope, a lasting impression on our hearts. That the good ship *Pandora* and all her gallant crew may escape the perils of the deep, and before many months have elapsed show her number, some early day, at Spithead, is the wish of their friends residing on the rock of the West.

,, 23rd. Eveline H. Buffett born.

,, 28th. Isaac Godfrey Christian born.

Aug. 9th. The inhabitants are slowly recovering from the epidemic which has pervaded the island during the last month. So general was the attack, that the public school has been discontinued, and public service but once performed on each Sabbath, in consequence. The teacher being fully employed attending the sick.

1849. Aug. 11th. Arrived, H. M. S. *Daphn*, Capt. Fanshawe, from Valparaiso, viâ Callao, bringing the *desiderata* of the community, viz., a bull, cow, and some rabbits. They were landed without any difficulty by our own boats. We also received from the Rev. Mr. Armstrong several boxes of acceptable articles, and a large case of books from the Christian Knowledge Society. At 3 P.M., Capt. Fanshawe and a party of the officers landed. At sunset they returned on board again, except the surgeon, who remained on shore at the particular request of Mr. Nobbs, who required some advice about the sick. Aug. 12th. At 1 P.M., Capt. Fanshawe returned on shore with a fresh party of officers, and attended Divine service. Much persuasion was used by our young people to induce Capt. F. to remain another day, but he told them he could not do so with propriety. At sunset, they all returned on board, and H. M. S. *Daphne* sailed for Tahiti. Capt. F. (as well as his officers) treated those of our people who went on board most kindly, and made most minute inquiries into our wants and actual condition. They were pleased to express their satisfaction at what they saw and heard, and left us deeply impressed with their courtesy and urbanity. May Almighty God have them in his holy keeping!

1849. Aug. 25th. Some of the inhabitants have had a relapse; at four P.M. Arthur Quintal, senior, fell from a rock, and injured himself badly, particularly the higher ribs and the thighs, as well as his left arm; he was conveyed home in a canoe; through the night he suffered much.

,, 30th. Arthur Quintal still suffers from his fall the other day; the major part of the inhabitants are sick; probably they have received an accession of disease from the barque *Elizabeth Archer*, from Sydney, which touched here a few days ago, some of her passengers being sick at the time, and our epidemic has assumed a very different type.

,, 31st. Frederick Young attacked with spasmodic affection of the stomach, which very nearly deprived him of life; had not the teacher been on the spot at the time, and the appropriate medicine (ether, brandy, and laudanum) within reach, in all human probability Frederick Young would have expired under the attack.

Sept. 4th. Maria Quintal delivered of a male child; the number of sick on the increase; the school discontinued, and only one service on the Sabbath, partly from the ill health of the teacher, and partly from the continual demand for his services night and day.

,, 6th. A large hair seal captured on the

1849. west side of the island. Fletcher Christian first discovered it among the rocks, and was much alarmed at the sight of it; he feared to go near it, lest it should be a ghost (of which he has a great horror), or some beast of prey, but quickly ascended the hill which overlooks the town, and gave the alarm; some persons went over to his assistance, and shot the animal just as it was making its retreat into the sea.

Sept. 11th. The infant born on the 4th was baptized, not being expected to live.

„ 12th. This morning the infant died; almost every one is affected with a most distressing cough. A remittant fever, attended with slight rigours, and much prostration of strength, is the type of the disease at present.

„ 20th. This day was set apart as a day of fasting and prayer. Public service commenced at eleven A.M., and ended at one P.M.; all who could get to church attended. Text, Romans, 2nd chapter, 4th and 5th verses. One of the females fainted during service.

Oct. 3rd. Hannah Quintal born.

„ 21st. Abigail Leah Christian born.

„ 28th. Lucy Anne Hagar Christian born.

Dec. 1st. Reuben Nobbs embarked in the brig *Georgia* for Valparaiso.

„ 20th. Eliza S. Adams born.

Summary.

1849. Number of births this year, 10; death, 1; marriage, 1. Inhabitants: males, 76; females, 79. 47 children attend the school, and 30 attend the Sunday-school. This year is unprecedented in the annals of Pitcairn's Island. We have been visited by two British men-of-war, the *Pandora*, Capt. Wood, and the *Daphne*, Capt. Fanshawe. The commanders of these ships and their officers treated the inhabitants with the greatest kindness, and were pleased to express their entire approval of all they saw and heard. The *Daphne* brought us a bull and cow, and some rabbits, with a variety of other articles, from the Rev. Mr. Armstrong and other friends in Valparaiso. The cattle and the rabbits produced a great sensation. Another (to us) wonderful occurrence is the arrival of so many other ships under English colours, viz., eight from the Australian colonies, bound for California, and one whaling vessel from London; in all nine merchantmen and two ships of war. American ships have dwindled down to seven—six whalers, and one from California; in her Reuben E. Nobbs embarked for Valparaiso. George Adams saved the life of a child alongside a ship in the

1849. offing. The inhabitants, with scarcely one exception, have suffered from sickness very severely during the months of August, September, and October. The school was discontinued, the children being too sick to attend, and the teacher was fully (and thank God efficiently) employed in ministering from house to house. Some of the cases were quite alarming, and the disease (the influenza) in general was more severe, but considerably modified from that of former years; violent spasms in the stomach and epigastric region were frequent in all stages of the complaint. At the close of the year, the inhabitants are enjoying much better health. May the recent affliction teach us to number our days, that we may apply our hearts unto wisdom!

1850. Jan. 1st. Arthur Quintal elected magistrate. Thursday O. Christian and Edward Quintal, councillors.

,, 6th. Robert Young born.

,, 23rd. This day was observed as the anniversary of the settlement of this colony, sixty years since. One survivor of that strange event and sanguinary result witnessed its celebration. At daylight one of the *Bounty*'s guns was discharged, and awakened the sleeping echoes and the more drowsy of its inhabitants. At ten A.M. Divine service was

1850. performed. After the sermon, the various letters received from the British Government and principal friends, were read from the pulpit and commented upon. At twelve o'clock (noon) a number of musketeers assembled under the flagstaff, and fired a volley in honour of the day. After dinner males and females assembled in front of the church (where the British flag was flying), and gave three cheers for Queen Victoria, three for the Government at home, three for the magistrate here, three for absent friends, three for the ladies, and three for the community in general, amid the firing of muskets and ringing of the bell. At sunset the gun of the *Bounty* was again fired, and the day closed in harmony and peace both towards God and man. It is voted that an annual celebration be observed.

I have (through the kindness of several gentlemen at the Foreign Office and the Admiralty, both at Whitehall and Somerset House) managed to procure the reports to the Admiralty, of the several commanders of H. M. ships, who have visited Pitcairn's Island, in order to show the general conduct of this virtuous little colony; as well I hope, in a manner of speaking, to show that I have not written about them in too praiseworthy a manner, which I consider is almost impossible.

[Copy.]

Report of Captain Sir Thomas Staines.

"H. M. S. *Britain*, Valparaiso, Oct. 18th, 1814.

"Sir,—I have the honour to inform you that, on my passage home from the Marquesas Islands to this port, on the morning of the 17th September, I fell in with an island where none is laid down, either in the Admiralty or other charts, according to the several chronometers of *Britain* and *Tagus*. I, therefore, hove-to until daylight, and then closed, to ascertain whether it was inhabited, which I soon discovered it to be, and to my great astonishment found that every individual on the island (forty in number) spoke very good English! They prove to be the descendants of the deluded crew of the *Bounty*, which from Tahiti proceeded to the above mentioned island, where the ship was burnt. Christian appeared to have been the leader and sole cause of the mutiny in that ship. A venerable old man, named John Adams, is the only surviving Englishman of those who last quitted Otahite in her, and whose exemplary conduct and fatherly care of the whole of the little colony, could not but command admiration. The pious manner in which all those born on the island have been reared, the correct sense of religion which has been instilled into their young minds by this old man, has given him the pre-eminence over the whole of them, to whom they look up as the father of the whole and one family. A son of Christian's was the first born upon the island, now about twenty-five years of age, namely, Thursday October Christian. The elder Christian fell a sacrifice to the jealousy of an Otahitian man, within three or four years after their arrival on the island. They were accompanied thither by six Otahitian men and twelve women, the former were all swept away by desperate contentions between them and the Englishmen, and five of the latter had died at different periods, leaving at present only one man and seven women of the original settlers. The island must undoubtedly be that called Pitcairn's, although erroneously laid down in the charts; we had the meridian sun close to it, which gave us 25° 48' for the latitude, and longitude by chronometers of *Britain* and *Tagus* 130° 25' west. It is abundant in yams, plantains, hogs, goats, and fowls; but affords no shelter for a ship or vessel of any description, neither could a ship water there without great difficulty. I cannot, however, refrain from offering my opinion, that it is well worthy the attention of our laudable religious societies, especially that for propagating the Christian religion; the whole of the inhabitants speaking the Otahitian tongue as well as English. During the whole of the time they have been on the island, only one ship has ever communicated with them, which took place about six years ago, an American ship, called the *Topaz* of Boston, Mayhew Folger, master. The island is completely iron bound with rocky shores, and landing in boats is at all times difficult, although safe to approach to within a short distance in a ship.

"I have the honour to be, Sir, your most obedient humble servant,

"(Signed)   T. STAINES.
" To Manley Dixon, Esq., Vice-Admiral of the Blue,
    " Commander in Chief, &c., &c., &c.,
        " Rio de Janeiro."

In Captain Beechy's report of Pitcairn's Island, December, 1825, he says, that when Pitcairn's Island was reported to be in sight from his ship, "every person came upon deck, the excitement and interest was so great. Shortly afterwards a boat, containing old Adams and eight of the islanders, came alongside. But before they ventured to take hold of the ship, they inquired if they might come on board; and upon permission being granted, they sprang up the side, and shook every officer by the hand with undisguised feelings of gratification. It was the first time Adams had been on board a ship of war since the mutiny, and his mind naturally reverted to scenes that could not fail to produce a temporary embarrassment, heightened, perhaps, by the familiarity with which he found himself addressed by persons of a class with those whom he had been accustomed to obey. Their dress, made up of the presents which had been given them by the masters and seamen of merchant and whale ships, was a perfect caricature. It was many hours after they came on board, before the ship could get near the island, during which time they so ingratiated themselves with us, that we felt the greatest desire to visit their houses, and rather than pass another night at sea, we put off in the boats, though at a considerable distance from the land, and accompanied them on shore. The difficulty of landing was more than repaid by the friendly reception we met with on the beach from Hannah Young, a very interesting young woman, the daughter of Adams. It appeared that John Buffett, who was a sea-faring man, ascertained the ship was a man-of-war, and not exactly knowing why, became so alarmed for the safety of Adams, that he either could not or would not answer any of the interrogations which were put to him. This mysterious silence set all the party in tears, as they feared he had discovered something adverse to their patriarch. At length his obduracy yielded to their entreaties; but before he explained the cause of his conduct, the boats were seen to put off from the ship, and Hannah immediately hurried to the beach to kiss the old man's cheek, which she did with a fervency demonstrative of the warmest affection. Before long we were all summoned to a hot supper, which consisted of a pig. Welcome, cheer, hospitality, and good humour, were the characteristics of the feast; and never was their beneficial influence more practically exemplified than on this occasion, by the demolition of nearly all that was placed before us. The next morning, when we were about to get up, the women, anxious to show their attentions, assembled to wish us good morning, and to inquire in what manner they could best contribute to our comforts, and to present us with some little gift, which the produce of the island afforded. All that remains to be said of these excellent people is, that they appear to live together in perfect harmony and contentment; to be virtuous, religious, cheerful, and hospitable beyond the limits of prudence; to be patterns of conjugal and parental affection; and to have no vices. We remained with them many days, and their unreserved manners gave us the fullest opportunity of becoming acquainted with any faults they might have possessed."

"Pitcairn's Island, March 17, 1830.
" On the 15th of March, I landed at this island, and was friendly and hospitably received by George Nobbs and all the inhabitants. My officers and men were most kindly treated at breakfast and dinner, and slept in their houses. My crew received a supply of cocoanuts and fruits. I had the gratification to hear William Quintal say part of the catechism, and answer several questions as to his knowledge of the redemption in Christ, and of the different habits of the Jews, their sects and diseases, perfectly, clearly, and distinctly, showing that he understood their meaning. I also heard two little girls repeat part of a hymn, which showed to me how well they had been instructed; and, lastly, I attended at their evening prayers. I can only trust that the God who preserves this island and its inhabitants from foreign injury, may keep them alive in the true faith of Jesus Christ in purity and peace, so that each person, at his death, may quit this world in the expectation of being for ever in heaven, through the merits of Jesus Christ. It was with very great satisfaction that I observed the Christian simplicity of these

natives. They appeared to have no guile. Their cottages were open to all, and all were welcome to their food; the pig—the fowl was killed and dressed instantly —the beds were ready—each was willing to show any and every part of the island; and to any question put by myself or Mr. Watson, as to the character and conduct of any individual, the answer was, "If it could do any good to answer you, I would; but as it cannot, it is wrong to tell tales." They repeatedly informed me that there were eighty-one souls on the island; but after frequent counting, we only reckoned seventy-nine. One quietly gave the Christian names of two others, but declined saying who their parents were, as "It would be wrong to tell my neighbour's shame." Before they began a meal, all joined hands in the attitude of prayer, with eyes raised to heaven, and one recited a simple grace, grateful for the present food, but beseeching spiritual nourishment. Each answered Amen, and after a pause the meal began; at the conclusion, another grace was offered up. Should any one arrive during the repast, all ceased to eat—the new guest said grace, to which each repeated Amen, and then the meal continued.

" (Signed)   WM. WALDEGRAVE,
" Capt. of H. M. S. *Seringapatam.*

" I hereby certify this is a true copy.
" (Signed)   F. D. BENNETT."

[Copy.]

"H. M. S. *Challenger*, May 30th, 1833.

"Sir,—After visiting several of the islands, I proceeded to Pitcairn's. The ship was immediately visited by most of the islanders, who came off in their canoes to invite the officers on shore. They were all well dressed, and in every respect had the appearance of Englishmen. I was sorry to find that they were not improved by their visit to Tahiti; but, on the contrary, I had reason to think they were much altered; and that on their return they had indulged in intemperance, by distilling a spirit from the ti-root, which grows in great quantities on the island. I interrogated the most intelligent of the men respecting their return to the island, and they unanimously agreed that they had never been happy or contented since they quitted it; and that nothing would have induced them to do so, excepting the fear of displeasing the British Government, which they feared they might have done, had they not profitted by the means offered to remove themselves; but, that now being re-established there, they would ever remain. They had nothing to complain of respecting their treatment at Tahiti; but appeared to have disliked the characters of the people, and were alarmed at the sickness which prevailed among them, and which altogether has carried off seventeen, five having died since their return. I found on the island a Mr. Joshua Hill, a gentleman nearly seventy years of age, who appears to have come from England expressly to establish himself amongst these people as a kind of pastor or monitor. He had not been on the island more than two or three months, and was officiating as schoolmaster, and had quite succeeded in supplanting the Englishman who had acted previously in that situation. He informed me on his arrival, he had found the island in the greatest state of irregularity. He landed on a Sunday, when he found Nobbs, who acted as their pastor, intoxicated, and in such a state from the effects of drunkenness, as to be incapable of performing his duties; and he had taken them upon himself, wishing to render as much service as possible to the islanders. It appeared to me so extraordinary a circumstance—a gentleman of Mr. Hill's age and apparent respectability, coming from England for the express purpose of residing upon Pitcairn's Island—that I at first thought he must be some adventurer, more likely to do harm than good, in the cause he had undertaken; but from the papers he showed me, he having been in communication with my Lords Commissioners of the Admiralty, the Colonial Office, Capt. Barclay, and many respectable gentlemen, offering his services, in the first instance, to remove the people from the island when it was first proposed, I was induced to think he must be interested about them; and as he had succeeded in restoring them to some kind of order, by putting a stop to the intemperance which existed, as he had broken up all their stills, and had formed them into a Temperance Society, I gave him all the assistance in my power to support him in his situation; the other Englishman having clearly proved by his conduct, that he was unfit for it. The number of people on the island at present is seventy-nine, and there appears to be abundance of vegetables of every description. They appeared to be under no alarm respecting a want of water, as they said, as their numbers increased, they must dig more reservoirs and wells. With respect to food, I am satisfied the island is capable of supporting 1000 persons. The soil is particularly good; and as most part of it is uncultivated, there is little fear of a scarcity. On their return from Tahiti, they found the island overrun with wild hogs, and their plantations destroyed, and they had only just succeeded in hunting them down; but even in their present state they were enabled to supply the *Challenger* with a large quantity of vegetables. Nothing could exceed the kindness of the people in offering everything they had, which they thought would be acceptable. It is impossible for any person to visit this island without being pleased with a people generally so amiable, springing from so guilty a stock, and brought up in so extraordinary a manner; and, although I have no hesitation in saying that I think they have lost much of that simplicity of character which has been represented of them by former visitors, they are still a well-disposed, well-behaved, kind, hospitable people, and if well advised and instructed, could be led to anything. But, I fear, if much left to themselves, and visited by many ships, which now is not an uncommon occurrence, what simplicity they have left will soon vanish, and they will partake of the characters of their neighbours, the Tahitians. The present generation of children is the finest I ever saw, and out of the whole number, seventy-nine, there are fifty-three under twenty years of age; and they appear to have been well instructed, many of them capable of reading, and nearly on a par with children of the same age in England. It certainly is desirable that they should have some better instruction. A clergyman would be most desirable and most acceptable to them, if any means could be adopted to appoint one. These people require many articles of clothing and household utensils, which the Government have sent them from time to time, and which they might be induced to repeat. Some articles they very much require. The *Challenger* took for them from Sydney some few things, but so scanty an allowance, that but very little benefit could be felt from it. I remained off the island two days, the ship being underweigh, as their Lordships are aware there is no anchorage, and the landing is particularly hazardous; it being very rarely that a ship's boat ought to land. The natives are very clever with their canoes, and will land in almost any weather. Having given all the assistance and advice in my power on the island, and arranged their little disputes to the best of my abilities, I left this little colony, being much prepossessed in their favour by everything I had seen, sincerely trusting that they may continue to live in that state of innocence and contentment they did previous to their departure for Tahiti; which, it is to be hoped, they may, if they do not return to the use of that spirit they have so well learned the art of distilling, and which was brought about by the Englishmen, a specimen of which I obtained. It was not unlike whisky, and very good.

"I am, sir, your obedient servant, &c., &c., &c.

"(Signed)   CHAS. H. FREEMANTLE,
"*Captain.*

"To Capt. the Hon. Geo. Elliott, Secretary,
"&c., &c., &c., Admiralty."

The late Lieut. James Lowry's Visit to Pitcairn's Island,
1839, in H. M. S. Sparrow-hawk.

"You may recollect that Pitcairn's Island was the one that Christian ran the *Bounty* on, after the mutiny, and then destroyed her; and that nothing was heard of them till 1814, when Sir T. Staines visited it by chance in the *Britain*, and his surprise was, as you may suppose, great, when he found it inhabited by people speaking English, and still greater, when he found from whence the stock sprung. At the time of his visit there were forty-five on the island, mostly children. There remained then but one of the mutineers alive, by the name of Adams (*alias* Smith), and from his exemplary manner in bringing his little flock up so religiously, he was not removed; the rest (with the exception of Young, the midshipman, who died on the island, and one who committed suicide) had been murdered by the men that they brought from Otaheite, who themselves were murdered by the women, to revenge the loss of the English, to whom they were very much attached. At the time of our visit, they had increased to 102 (51 males and 51 females), a great part of them children, and as fine a race as ever I saw.

Some of the girls and young women were very pretty, and would be considered beauties in Old England, and all were good-looking. There was but one ever born on the island with any defect in his person, and that was only in his eye. The island is a beautiful little spot, and I doubt if there is any in the world of the size to equal it in scenery or fertility. It is not quite one square mile in extent, and was supposed capable of maintaining 1000 inhabitants. When first taken possession of, it was divided into seven equal parts, the number of English at that time on the island. It has since been subdivided, as the families have increased; still, there is plenty, and for some generations to come, as but a small part is cultivated, and a great part of the produce they supply to whalers, in exchange for cloths or any necessary articles they want—money there being of no value. They have plenty of fowls, pigs, and goats, as well as fruits and vegetables, and their yams are the finest I ever saw; we got a plentiful supply from them in exchange for articles that we took them. It is a good thing for them that there is no anchorage, as they stand less chance of being corrupted by communication with the crews of the whale ships—the only ones that ever touch there, except the yearly man-of-war. We remained four days longer than any ship of war ever stayed before, and much pleased we were with them. You could not, in fact, be otherwise, as I doubt if, in the same number, you would find so few exceptions to good moral behaviour. They all came down to receive us on landing, and conducted us to their houses—all anxious

for us to go with them; and they had provided their
best. There were six or seven in the first party, so we
were divided pretty well all over the island. Before all
meals they offer up thanks, and they nearly put us to
the blush—if a blush was to be found amongst us—
when they first dined on board, as some did daily, by
asking us, after waiting some time, if we never said
grace; and on our replying but seldom, they asked
permission to do so before they would begin. There is
not such another happy little community in the world.
On their first rising, they assemble and sing the Morning
Hymn; and, before retiring, they again assemble and
sing the Evening Hymn. A few trifling quarrels they
had, which the captain settled to their satisfaction.
They have also made a small code of laws, and one of
their punishments is flogging with a cat-o'-nine tails for
theft; only once had they occasion to use it. There are
but two staying on the island that were not born there,
and they are Englishmen, and they now will not admit
any more. These two have resided there a long time,
and have families. One of them acts as schoolmaster
and parson; in return, the rest of the males cultivate his
land. We all visited the school, and were much pleased
with their progress; the seniors could write and read,
and understand arithmetic. All now on the island can
read, which they could not do formerly for want of
books, as they had for many years but one Bible amongst
them. I was not on shore on Sunday; but, from the
accounts of those that were, it must have been a very
gratifying sight. All attend; no manner of work is

done, not even meals cooked, that being provided on Saturdays. They did not forget, in their prayers, our little Queen, and all people in England. The service was of the Church of England. Their marriages take place early—generally the girls at fourteen or fifteen, and the men under twenty. One of the girls at the school, who was only fifteen, had been married for upwards of twelve months, and has one child. There has been only one old maid on the island, and she is now nearly fifty, and is as cross and crabbed as any old maid need be; she rails against the early marriages most heartily. Their manner of living is so simple, that they have few diseases, and deaths rarely visit them except from old age. There are thirteen families, who live in comfortable houses, constructed of wood. One end is partitioned off for the bedroom of the father and mother of the flock, with bed places along one side of the wall, facing the door of the other apartment. They are not very clean in their houses, but that could be easily remedied if they had any lady to put them in the way of cleanly habits. They have neither fleas, bugs, lice, or any poisonous reptile whatever on the island. The admiral and his wife sent them a present of carpenters' tools, needles, thread, and some cottons for gowns, and there were some books sent from England; and I am sure, if it was known in Old England what an interesting little community they are, their wants would be well supplied by every opportunity. The women and girls dress in a loose sort of dressing-gown, not confined at the waist, and coming up close to the neck. Neither sex wear shoes, although the females have pretty little feet of their own; and the present generation have good hair. The first families were curly, but it has gradually become the same as Europeans'. When they have no visitors, they have meat but twice a-week, plenty of vegetables at all times, and they only drink water and cocoa-nut milk. They have plenty of goats; but never milk them, letting them run wild to breed. Some years ago, they managed to distil a spirit which made them all drunk; when, after a short time, they felt it hurt the constitution, they made a law that no more should be made, since which time drunkenness has not been known on the island.

"They have no springs, but have plenty of water from the rain, having now several reservoirs. About eight or nine years ago, they were greatly in want of it, partly by cleaning them, as they would not hold water for two or three years after, they having removed the sluice, &c., that kept it in. They then applied to Government for a vessel to remove them, when they sent the *Comet* to take them to Otaheite. After a stay there for a short time, they were so disgusted with their lewd manner of living, that they got the consul to send them back again; and it has done them this good, that they will not again be anxious to leave their happy little spot; and they themselves seem quite aware that they are far better off and happier than the generality of mankind. The island was inhabited at some former period, as stone adzes, idols, and several other things that savages are in the habit of using, have been found there. Little is now left of the *Bounty*, as every one that touches there tries to get a part of her. I got a small piece of wood, which I have made into a box, and a part of her keel. Little more have I to say of this interesting spot. On our leaving, all followed us to the beach to see us off, with many kind wishes for our health, and a happy return to our friends in England. Such was our parting from, I think, the most interesting little spot in the world."

Captain J. Wood's Report, dated August 3rd, 1849.

"I FOUND these most interesting people the same thriving, industrious, simple, and happy community they have ever been represented; the population rapidly increasing, and the smallness of their island the only complaint.

"Tahiti, Jan. 30, 1850.

"MY LORD,—I have the honour to transmit to your Lordship herewith, the copies of two letters, dated the 14th instant, which I have received from Pitcairn's Island, stating that, notwithstanding the increasing necessity for the removal of the surplus population of that island, the community could not at present overcome their reluctance to separate, or yet decide which amongst them should be the first to leave their homes.

"I have, &c. &c.
"(Signed) G. C. MILLER.
"The Viscount Palmerston, G.C.B.,
"&c. &c. &c."

[Copy.]

"Pitcairn's Island, Jan. 14th, 1850.

"HONOURED SIR,—I embrace this opportunity of sending a few lines, being sensible of the interest you take in our little community. I trust you will not be offended at my again addressing you. I wrote to your honour by H. M. S. *Daphne;* since that time there has been no alteration in the views of the inhabitants. The fact is, they will not emigrate till obliged to by sheer necessity. About two months since a young man, the son of Mr. Nobbs, left here for Valparaiso, to endeavour to get employment as a clerk, or any situation by which he may support himself, he being a cripple, and not fitted for any laborious employment. As I before remarked, the inhabitants will not remove until driven by necessity; that time, I presume, is not very far distant. The number at present is—males, 76; females, 79. Ten births last year, and one death—an infant. About ten couple are now marriageable, and the increase will be rapid. I thank you, Sir, in the name of the community, for your kindness and well-wishes towards us, and *should esteem it a great favour*, should an opportunity offer, if you would send us a fig-tree and a rose-tree.

"I am, Sir, &c.

" (Signed)   J. BUFFETT.

" G. C. Miller, Esq.
   "British Consul, Tahiti."

"Pitcairn's Island, Jan. 14th, 1850.

"Sir,—An opportunity offering, I gladly embrace it (in the name of the community), to return you our unqualified thanks for the solicitude you have so kindly evinced in our behalf. The very secluded position of Pitcairn's Island prevents our communicating often with our friends, of whose untiring benevolence we are so frequently the recipients, and right glad are we to reckon yourself and your honourable and gallant uncle among the number.

Whether any of my people will avail themselves of the various offers made them, as regards emigrating, I cannot at present say definitely; for although the necessity exists, and its imperative demands cannot be much longer avoided, such is the affection existing between the members of this unique society, that they are intent only upon putting off the "evil day" of separation. Another cause, and that not a slight one is the great and paramount influence the French are exercising in these seas. Now, to persons whose manners, customs, and every idea are intrinsically "English," to be obliged to succumb to the dictates of those against whom an instinctive dislike has been implanted in their breasts, by their ancestors of the *Bounty*, is more than a trifle. Here they enjoy the favour and protection of the British Government; and though often put to great straits, and the difficulties are daily increasing, yet they will, I presume, remain for some time to come, where they can, amid all their privations, worship God without molestation, and behold, on Sundays and other occasions, the British flag wave over their isolated and rocky abode. They had not, when I wrote to the Consul General some time ago, so serious a consideration as they have since; and when the generous offer made them by your honourable uncle and other gentlemen in Oahu, and, through your kind solicitude, by the chiefs of the Society Islands, came to their knowledge, and they began to inquire which among them would avail themselves of the very favourable and disinterested invitations, their hearts failed them; they could not brook the idea of separation, and settled down to their accustomed avocations, until the suggestions of their necessities should become more peremptory.* Will you be pleased, worthy Sir, to prepresent our grateful acknowledgements to the Rev. Mr. Barff, and the chiefs before mentioned; and though we do not profit by their generosity, we appreciate it not the less.

"Hoping that you may many years fill the important situation which gives you so many opportunities of practical benevolence, permit me, respected friend, to subscribe myself,

"Your much obliged and grateful servant,
"(Signed)   GEORGE H. NOBBS,
"Pastor.
"In the name, and on behalf, of the community of Pitcairn's Island.
"To G. C. Miller, Esq.
"British Consul, Tahiti."

* If these natives could be removed in a body, to some un-

"Foreign Office, Sept. 12th, 1850.

"SIR,—I am directed by Viscount Palmerston to transmit to you the copy of a despatch from Her Majesty's Consul at Tahiti, with the copies of two letters General Miller had received from Pitcairn's Island, stating that, notwithstanding the increasing necessity for the removal of the surplus population of that island, the community could not, at present, overcome their reluctance to separate, or yet decide which amongst them should be the first to leave their homes. And I am to request that, in laying the papers before Earl Grey, you will move his Lordship to cause an inquiry to be made, and to ascertain whether all the plants and vegetables which would grow upon Pitcairn's Island have been sent thither; as it would appear from their request for a fig and rose tree, that such has not been done. I am further directed by Viscount Palmerston to suggest for the consideration of Earl Grey, that instructions should be sent by the Admiralty to the officer in command of H. M. ships in the Pacific, to take such opportunities as may occur to visit Pitcairn's Island, and to convey to the inhabitants such plants and seeds as may be useful to them. The plants and

<small>inhabited island, they would like the change, but some three or four of the elder families would not leave the island under any circumstances. Juan Fernandez is where they want much to go to, which might be obtained from the Chilian Government, and they would in that case be under the eye of the Admiral of the Valparaiso station, these islands being only 250 miles from there.—ED.</small>

seeds might be obtained for this purpose from the Royal Gardens at Kew, or from the Horticultural Gardens at Chiswick.

"(Signed.)   H. U. ADDINGTON,
"*Secretary of the Colonial Office.*"

I shall make no comments upon the following correspondence between Joshua Hill, George Nobbs, John Buffett, and John Evans, and the British Admiral of the South West American station; but allow my readers to judge for themselves the awkward position in which these islanders were placed for many months by the said Joshua Hill.

"H. M. S. *Spartiate*, Rio de Janeiro,
"Sept. 3rd, 1833.

"SIR,—I herewith transmit, for the information of the Lords Commissioners of the Admiralty, copies of letters addressed to me by the Right Honourable Lord James Townshend, the senior officer in the Pacific, with copies of letters from Mr. White, H. M. Consul General for Chili, and from a Mr. Joshua Hill, a resident on Pitcairn's Island. In submitting these documents for the consideration of their Lordships, I beg leave to state, that it is my intention, whenever a ship can possibly be spared from the more urgent duties of the station, to cause the several islands in the Pacific to be visited. But with regard to the removal from Pitcairn's Island of the individuals of whom Mr. Joshua Hill complains,

I have to request their Lordships will be pleased to acquaint me how far such an act may be justifiable; provided the majority of the inhabitants should express their wishes to that effect, and the Captain of the ship visiting the island considers such a measure would be beneficial to the harmony and prosperity of the community in general.

"I am, Sir,
"&c., &c., &c.,
"(Signed.)   MICHAEL SEYMOUR,
"*Rear Admiral.*

"To Capt. the Hon. George Elliott, C.B.,
"Admiralty."

"H. M. S. *Dublin*,
"27th June, 1833.

"SIR,—I transmit the copy of a letter from His Majesty's Consul General for Chili, with its enclosure, stating the complaint of a Mr. Joshua Hill, who it appears is a resident on Pitcairn's Island. The Consul General's letter was delivered to me, after the ship was under weigh at Valparaiso, on the 23rd inst.; so that I had no opportunity of making any further inquiry of him on this subject; and, as I have never before heard of the circumstances, all I can now do is to transmit the correspondence to you, with a remark, that this adds one more to the list of grievances, which appears to me (and which I have often repeated to Sir Thomas

Baker) to call for the appearance of one of H. M. ships among the islands of the Pacific.

"I have the honour to be, &c., &c.,
"(Signed.) J. TOWNSHEND,
"*Captain and Senior Officer.*
"To Rear Admiral Sir Michael Seymour,
"Commander-in-Chief, &c., &c."

"British Consulate,
"Valparaiso, June 24th, 1833.

"SIR,—I have the honour to enclose a copy of a letter I received yesterday from a Mr. Joshua Hill, residing upon Pitcairn's Island, complaining of some Englishmen resident here, creating dissenticns among the natives, and requesting they may be taken from the island. Whether Mr. Joshua Hill has any authority from His Majesty's Government to interfere with the affairs of the island, I am not informed; but, knowing that His Majesty's Government takes a warm interest in the welfare of these people of Pitcairn's Island, I submit His request to your Lordship's consideration, presuming that you have the power to exercise your authority in this particular case.

"I have the honour, &c., &c.,
"(Signed.) J. WHITE,
"*His Majesty's acting Consul General.*
"To Rt. Hon. Lord J. Townshend, &c."

"Pitcairn's Island, March 25th, 1833.
"SIR,—I had the honour of addressing you a few lines

by Capt. Fremantle, R. N., of H. M. S. *Challenger*, recently sailing hence for your port and England, since when I have experienced considerable trouble by the presence of two or three foreigners, of whom I made mention, residing upon the island; and till they are compelled to leave it, there will no peace be upon Pitcairn's. I have again written home to our Government on the subject, as well as to Capt. Fremantle, that his sentence whilst here, for them to leave the island as soon as possible, will never be respected by these men. Let me beg and pray of you, Sir, for the sake of these natives, that the British Commander in Chief, the Right Honourable Lord James Townshend may be intreated to consider the case, and that he would be pleased to give the necessary directions for the removal of these foreigners (Englishmen) from this in other respects happy little island.

"I have the honour to be, &c., &c., &c.,
" (Signed.) Joshua Hill.
" John White, Esq.; British Consul, &c.,
"Valparaiso."

[Copy.]
" H. M. S. *Blonde*, Valparaiso, Dec. 4th, 183 .
" Sir,—I beg to transmit, for the information of my Lords Commissioners of the Admiralty, a number of documents, brought by Capt. Seymour in the *Challenger*, relative to Pitcairn's Island. Mr. Hill appears to have assumed a power, and exercised a severity, and even cruelty, at Pitcairn's Island quite unauthorized. It is

much to be regretted that that once exemplary and interesting population should be under the influence of such a man. I am, &c., &c., &c.

"(Signed.)   T. MASON,
"*Commander.*"

"Capt. the Hon. Geo. Elliott, C.B.,
"Admiralty."

[Copy.]

"Tahiti, August 13th, 1831.

"THE whole of the people belonging to Pitcairn's Island having mutually agreed to receive Mr. Nobbs as their sole teacher and minister, we, whose names are undersigned, do hereby testify our approval of this arrangement, and do most sincerely hope that he may prove a great and extensive blessing to the whole of the inhabitants.

"(Signed)   G. PRITCHARD, H. B. M. Consul.
"H. NOTT, } Missionaries.
"CHAS. WILLSON,

"I hereby certify that this is a true Copy.

"(Signed.)   F. D. BENNETT."

[Copy.]

"*To all whom it may concern.*

"WE, the undersigned, heads of families at Pitcairn's Island, do hereby certify that Mr. George H. Nobbs has conducted himself to our satisfaction ever since he has been on this island; also, we have no fault to find with his manner of keeping school for the space of four years;

and the reason why Mr. Nobbs is dismissed from teaching and school-keeping is in consequence of a disagreement between Mr. Nobbs and Mr. Joshua Hill, who has lately come to reside on this island amongst us.

"Pitcairn's Island, Dec. 1832.

"(Signed.) Edward × Quintal.
         his mark.

"William × Young.
         his mark.

"John × Quintal.
         his mark.

"Arthur × Quintal.
         his mark.

"George × Adams.
         his mark.

"Charles × Christian.
         his mark.

"William × M'Coy.
         his mark.

"Fletcher × Christian.
         his mark.

"I hereby certify that this is a true copy.
"(Signed.)   F. D. Bennett."

"*The humble Petition of George Hann Nobbs, late Teacher at Pitcairn's Island.*

"Sheweth,—That your petitioner went to Pitcairn's Island in 1828, with the intention of assisting the late

John Adams in teaching and school-keeping; that, on your petitioner's arrival, he was kindly received by the natives, and, at their request, and with the consent of John Adams, your petitioner immediately commenced keeping school. On the death of John Adams your petitioner, at the desire of the natives, undertook the charge of their spiritual affairs, and your petitioner's conduct gave general satisfaction, as will appear by the accompanying certificate. For the space of two years things went on in an amicable manner, when H. M. S. *Comet* arrived, for the purpose of removing the inhabitants to Tahiti. After some deliberation, the natives determined to remove. Your petitioner, thinking he could be of no further service to them (as they would be under the guidance of the missionaries at Tahiti), wished to remain with his wife and family on the island of Pitcairn. This the islanders objected to, and insisted on your petitioner accompanying them to Tahiti. Your petitioner complied with their desires; and, previous to Capt. Sandilands (of H. M. S. *Comet*) quitting Tahiti, he (Capt. S.) sent for your petitioner, and told him he must not quit the Pitcairn people, but continue to be their teacher, under the direction of the missionaries: adding, " You have been of service to them, and may be so still; you are married amongst them, and in fact become as one of themselves; therefore you ought not, and it is my request you will not, leave them." After the departure of H. M. S. *Comet*, sickness appeared among the late inhabitants of the Pitcairn's, and ultimately twelve died. During their sickness the attention paid them by your petitioner obtained the approbation of the missionaries and other gentlemen residing in Tahiti. Your petitioner was also indefatigable in obtaining subscriptions to assist them in returning to their native land. Previous to their departure from Tahiti, they went, of their own accord, to the missionaries, and requested your petitioner should be appointed " their sole minister and teacher," which the missionaries agreed to, and signed a paper to that effect, a copy of which accompanies this petition.

"A short time after our return to Pitcairn's Island, some of the natives (Edward Quintal, William Young, and Fletcher Christian), determined to re-commence distilling rum—a practice they had been accustomed to in John Adams's time. Your petitioner remonstrated with them on the impropriety of their conduct, but to no purpose; the answer they gave to your petitioner's advice was—" We are our own masters; we shall do as we like; no one shall control us." Many times your petitioner talked with them, and begged them to desist from distilling spirits; but your petitioner always received abuse in return, and twice narrowly escaped a beating from Edward Quintal. Afterwards a Mr. Hill arrived, who assumed great authority, said he was sent out by the British Government to adjust the internal affairs of the island, and that the British ships of war on the coast were under his direction. He furthermore told the natives that he had resided for a considerable time at Oahu, where he possessed great influence, by reason that your Honour had served under him on board one of the Honourable East India Company's ships, which he (Mr. Hill) commanded. Believing these things to be true, your petitioner gave Mr. Hill an apartment in your petitioner's house, and used every means to make him comfortable; but, before one month had expired, Mr. Hill had succeeded, by villanous misrepresentations, atrocious falsehoods, and magnificent promises of presents, to be obtained through his influence from the British Government and several British of Mr. Hill's acquaintance, in ejecting your petitioner from his house. Mr. Hill then told the natives he should act as their teacher, until a qualified teacher was sent out from England. Soon after, H. M. S. *Challenger* touched at Pitcairn's Island from Tahiti. Capt. Freemantle assembled the inhabitants, and informed them that Mr. Hill was not acting under the authority of the British Government; also, that he, Capt. Freemantle, came on shore with the intention of removing Mr. Hill from the island; but, on hearing that your petitioner had partaken of the spirits distilled by the natives, he (Capt. F.) informed your petitioner that he could not re-instate him in the situation of which Mr. Hill had deprived him; at the same time Capt. F. told Mr. Hill he did not approve of his (Mr. H.'s) conduct, as he acted without authority. Capt. F. also told Mr. Hill he must not interfere with the laws, as the administration of them was vested in the natives. Capt. F. asked your petitioner what he intended to do. Your petitioner replied, it was his wish to leave the island. Capt. F. said he thought it was the best thing your petitioner could do, under existing circumstances, but that he certainly might remain if he chose. Before Capt. F. departed, he told the natives it was his belief that Mr. Hill wished to get the other Europeans off the island, that he, Mr. Hill, might make himself king over them. Capt. F. also sharply reprimanded Mr. Hill for calling the other British residents, "lousy foreigners," &c.; and bade him desist from doing so. Mr. Hill promised to obey, but never kept his promise. Shortly after Capt. F.'s departure, Mr. Hill began again to oppress your petitioner and the two other Englishmen. He ordered the natives to turn us out of their houses; and our nearest relatives dared not come and visit us. As soon as a ship appeared off the island, a canoe was despatched on board, forbidding the officers and crew coming to our houses, and we were threatened with stripes if we offered to go on board. In May last, an act was passed (by force) to deprive our children of their mothers' inheritance, merely because their fathers were foreigners (Englishmen). In August Mr. Hill sent his colleagues to seize the muskets of those persons whom, he said, were opposed to the governor of the commonwealth. As soon as Mr. Hill obtained possession of the muskets, he loaded them with powder and ball, and deposited them in his bedroom, for the use of the magistracy of the island. Every Sunday a loaded musket is placed beneath his seat in church, to intimidate his hearers. Since that period your petitioner has been in continued alarm for the lives of himself and family. Your petitioner dared not go out of his house after dark, nor up to his plantation at any time, by himself, for fear of being maltreated by the colleagues of Mr. Hill. Several of the natives protested against such conduct; Mr. Hill threatened to give them a flogging, and, moreover, said, that if they did not obey him, he would cause a military governor to be sent out from England, with a party of soldiers, who would take their land from them and treat them as slaves. In the month of November last your petitioner was seized with the dysentery, and for three months was confined to his bed. Your petitioner could not obtain medicine, although there was a medicine-chest on the island, and of which your petitioner was a part proprietor. In fact, it was the declared intent of Joshua Hill and his colleagues to bring about the death of your petitioner, either by hanging, flogging, or starvation.

"Your petitioner at last, by sickness, deprivation of common necessaries, and anxiety of mind, occasioned by Joshua Hill's wicked counsel and conduct, was brought to the verge of the grave, when, providentially, a ship appeared in sight, which proved to be the *Tuscan* of London, Capt. Stavers; who, on seeing the miserable condition of your petitioner, kindly consented, at your petitioner's earnest request, to give him a passage to Tahiti. Owing to the professional and benevolent endeavours of Dr. Bennett, surgeon of the *Tuscan*, your petitioner is recovering, and hopes, ere long, to be re-instated in health. And now, Honoured Sir, will you permit your unfortunate petitioner to implore your Honour's protection? Driven from family and home by an unauthorized person, without friends or money, and almost without clothes, your petitioner is at a loss what course to pursue. Your petitioner cannot support the idea of being separated for ever from his wife and family; but, alas! he can scarcely hope to see them again unless your Honour condescends to espouse his cause. Convinced that his cause is just, and knowing that Capt. Stavers and Dr. Bennett can corroborate the most material statements in this petition, the fervent prayer of your petitioner is, that your Honour would cause your petitioner, and the other two unfortunate Englishmen with him, to be restored to their families and possessions on Pitcairn's Island; and your petitioner, in duty bound, will ever pray, &c.

"Your petitioner has no desire to be replaced as teacher, but simply to employ himself in agricultural pursuits, for the support of his family."

[Copy.]

"HONOURED SIR,—I hope you will excuse the liberty I take in writing to you, which I doubt not you will, when you are informed in what critical circumstances I am placed. In December, 1823, on our return to England, we touched at Pitcairn's Island, and by desire of the natives and consent of our captain, I went on shore to teach their children to read, &c., which I did to their satisfaction. Mr. Nobbs arriving soon after, became their teacher; since then I have lived as a private individual, on good terms with the natives. After going to Tahiti with them, and remaining there about three weeks, I procured a passage for myself, my wife, and family, and arrived at Pitcairn's Island about three months before the rest of the natives. After they all arrived, we all lived together upon friendly terms, until the arrival of Mr. Joshua Hill from Tahiti, in October, 1832, who stated that he had been sent out by the British Government, and whatever he was in want of he would procure from England, New South Wales, or Valparaiso. By means of such promises, and by his making them believe that whatever heretofore has been sent out, was by his influence, he has gained the favour of a few natives, and appointed three elders and two privy councillors. He has framed laws and built a prison; and should any of the natives refuse to obey him, let his proposals be ever so unjust, he tells them he will send to England for a governor and a regiment of soldiers. By such means he has persuaded the natives to sign a petition to Government to deprive us Englishmen and our children of their lands; and I am ordered, with my wife and five children, to leave the island. His plea (J. H.'s) is, that there is not land sufficient. At the same time, he has proposed to send to England for English ladies, for wives for the youth of the island; and because I made known his plan of sending my wife and family off the island, I had a mock-trial, on which Mr. Hill was judge, jury, and executioner. After Mr. Hill's beating me over the head, breaking it in two places, likewise my finger, I was suspended by my hands in the church, and flogged until I was not able to walk home, and confined to my bed for two weeks, and it was several weeks before I was able to work or have the use of my hand; my wife, at the same time, was ill and not able to work, and Mr. J. Hill would not allow the natives to visit me or my wife, not even her own sister, but literally tried to starve us. Charles Christian, the oldest man on the island, was brutally treated, and turned out of his house, for trying to prevent my being flogged; and because the women assembled crying shame on his (Mr. J. H's.) proceedings, he, Mr. J. Hill, on the Sunday following read the riot act, and told them, should they do so again, the authorities would be justified in shooting them. He then sent his colleagues, as he is pleased to call them, to take possession of our fire-arms, which they loaded with ball, and Mr. J. Hill has since kept them in his possession. Since this, Sir, not only the lives of us English residents, but some of the natives, have been in danger from the malicious temper of Mr. J. Hill. He has been the means of depriving one of my children of the land left her by her grandfather, and he proposes to deprive the others also, and as they grow up to send them to sea as cabin boys, &c. He wished Capt. Fremantle, of H. M. S. *Challenger*, who touched at Pitcairn's Island, in February, 1832, to remove me from the island; but he (Capt. F.) would not. Since that he has been trying all in his power to prejudice the natives against me. Capt. T. Stavers has been so kind as to give me a passage to Tahiti, when I shall endeavour to get a passage for my family, either to Lord Howe's Island or Rappa. In the mean time, I humbly hope, Sir, you will use your influence to get Mr. Hill removed from Pitcairn's Island; it is the desire of most of the inhabitants. The land that Mr. Hill wishes to deprive my children of, is their mother's portion, left by her father (Edward Young of the *Bounty*). If, Sir, you would condescend to write me a few lines, informing me how to act, to the care of Mr. Pritchard, Tahiti, you would greatly oblige your most humble servant,

"(Signed)   J. BUFFETT."

[Copy.]

Extract of John Buffett's Sentence.

"Pitcairn's Island, 5th August, 1833.

"IT only remains with us to declare the sentence of the law, which is:—And this court doth accordingly adjudge, that you receive forthwith three dozen lashes with a cat, upon the bare back and breech, together with a fine of three barrels of yams or potatoes, to be paid within one month, or, in default thereof, an extra barrel will be required for this re-iterated contempt of court.

(Signed, &c., by the whole court.)

"Moreover, John Buffett, the sentence of the court is, that whether with or without your family, you are to leave this island by the first vessel that may present herself thus; for if you do not, punishment and imprisonment will be the consequence.

(Signed by the whole court.)

"N.B. And, moreover, it is resolved by the court that in case you, John Buffett, should presume to deviate from the re-iterated promise which you made to the said court, on the 5th instant, touching your future rule of action (*i. e.* good conduct and the assurances which you then made, duly to respect the public functionaries of this island), whilst thus you may remain upon it, that the residuum of your said punishment (twenty-four from thirty-six) shall be duly inflicted.

"But, on the contrary, it may be observed, *in limine*, that the executive, wishing always peace and tranquillity and good order, which, with the help of the blessed Lord, it has determined to maintain and enforce. In the event, therefore, of a manifest reformation of your rule of action and erroneous actions and principles, the executive is ever ready and willing to take into due consideration, so far as circumstances may permit, and may prove compatible with the general interest and welfare of the commonwealth, touching the premises, and in relation to the said rule of action which you may hereafter think just to pursue, and the good behaviour which circumstances render it expedient that you should adopt; otherwise, in due course, the said balance of a dozen or fourteen, which still remain due to you, must be settled accordingly."

(Signed, &c., aforesaid by the court.)

"I hereby certify that the foregoing are true

extracts and copies from the originals deposited in the archives.

" Pitcairn's Island, 5th August, 1833.
" (Signed)   J. HILL.

" To John Buffett, Pitcairn's Island."

"I hereby certify that this is a true copy.
" (Signed)   F. D. BENNETT."

[Copy.]
" <i>The Humble Petition of John Evans, two years resident on Pitcairn's Island.</i></div>

"SHEWETH,—That your petitioner landed on Pitcairn's in the year 1823, and after a residence of twelve months, was united in marriage with the second daughter of the late John Adams (by his consent). From that period your petitioner continued to live in peace and harmony with the natives, and maintained himself and family in a comfortable manner. Your petitioner accompanied the Pitcairn people to Tahiti, and while there, assisted them as much as lay in his power. At their return, the natives were perfectly agreeable that your petitioner should return with them, and resume possession of his wife's land, &c. Things went on in their usual train for twelve months after our return, when a Mr. Joshua Hill arrived at Pitcairn's, who informed your petitioner he was come by authority of the British Government to adjust the internal affairs of the island, and that he had sent orders to Valparaiso for H. M. S. *Dublin* to come and take him on board, and convey him to the Marquesas Islands in a diplomatic capacity. Your petitioner gave credit to Mr. Hill's assertions, and treated him with all possible respect, also cheerfully contributed to his support; but scarcely had Mr. Hill been on shore three weeks, when he attempted to persuade your petitioner's wife to leave him, saying he would take her under his protection, and supply her with everything she wanted; adding, 'I will cause the first captain of a man-of-war who arrives to remove these lousy foreigners from the island.' My wife refused to do as he wished, and from that time forth he became her declared enemy. Shortly after a ship of war arrived, the captain of which declared he knew nothing of Mr. Hill, neither had he (Mr. Hill) any authority from the British Government. Mr. Hill used every means in his power, by misrepresentation and gross falsehood, to induce Capt. Freemantle to remove me from the island. This Capt. F. refused, saying, he had a good opinion of me, and should not separate me from my family. Capt. Freemantle severely reprimanded Mr. Hill for his conduct towards the English residents, and desired him to alter his conduct towards them; this Mr. Hill promised to do, but malice and falsehood are prominent traits in the character of Joshua Hill. No sooner was Capt. Freemantle gone, than Mr. Hill (vexed that he had not gained his point) became more outrageous than ever; he still asserted he was sent out by the British Government, that Capt. F. was no gentleman, and denounced vengeance on every native that did not join with him in oppressing the lousy foreigners. Whenever a ship appeared in sight, two confidential men were despatched on board to forbid the captain and officers holding any communication with foreigners on shore; and we were prohibited, under pains and penalties, from going on board. In May last a prison was built, for the avowed purpose of confining the Englishmen and their friends, and a law passed (by force) depriving our children of their mothers' inheritance; and all the genuine natives, from seven years and upwards, were compelled to sign a paper, declaring they would never intermarry with the foreigners—a term applied to our children as well as ourselves. In July a law was enacted relative to high treason. Your petitioner requested a copy as a guide for his future conduct; Mr. Hill refused to give him one, flew into a violent rage, and shortly after, your petitioner was dragged to the church, underwent a mock-trial, no witnesses being allowed, and received one dozen lashes with a cat-o'-nine-tails, each tail being the size of a man's little finger. Your petitioner was so much hurt about the head, eyes, and ribs, as to be confined to his bed for ten days. From this time the state of things became desperate, and your petitioner was under continual alarm for the lives of himself and family. Mr. Hill and his colleagues were continually threatening the life of some one or other, and your petitioner firmly believes, had it not been for the opportune arrival of the ship *Tuscan*, Capt. R. T. Stavers, murder would have been shortly committed. Capt. Stavers, seeing the untoward state of affairs, humanely consented to give your petitioner a passage to Tahiti. And now, Honoured Sir, will you permit your petitioner to hope you will commiserate my unhappy condition? Neither the natives nor Mr. Hill can bring any serious charge against me, as Capt. Stavers and Dr. Bennett can certify, and yet your petitioner is banished from family and home, merely to gratify the malevolence of Mr. Hill. Your petitioner humbly begs that your Honour will restore your petitioner again to his wife and family, that he may support them by his labour.

"And your petitioner as in duty bound, will ever pray.*"

Copy of a Letter, dated Pitcairn's Island, 3rd October 1833, from the Public Functionaries and others, to Captain Joshua Hill, Teacher, &c.

"RESPECTED SIR.—We, the undersigned, being all public authorities, as well as other natives, who are earnestly desirous for the prosperity and welfare of our dearly beloved island, beg not only that you will be pleased to accept our most sincere gratitude for all which you have done for us, in various respects, both before your arrival here in October last, and since, especially in thus saving and snatching us so providentially, as it were, from the brink of infidelity itself, and as well as other crying and besetting sins (now too painful for us to contemplate), which otherwise must have been our entire and total

* The three letters of Buffett, Nobbs, and Evans, not being directed to any particular person, it is supposed that the direction was on the envelope only; but the Author believes them to be intended for the commander of H. M. naval forces, on the s.w. coast of America.

ruin. But, moreover, we entreat that you will not think of leaving us yet awhile, or until we become, with the blessed Lord's help, settled somewhat in safety. For, indeed, we have too good reason to know, that so long as one of these profligate foreigners is among us on Pitcairn's, we never shall be able to go on aright, or resist their corrupting or destructive practices. Hence we implore you, dear friend, to consider our unfortunate case; and remember that, on your arrival here (aforesaid), we had two cursed stills up—without a school, without a church!—and, alas! alas!—"tell it not in Gath"—we were living without God, in the world!

"We pray you, therefore, leave us not thus to the enemy, or we fear again that we shall be for ever lost!

"We hereto subscribe ourselves, respected Sir, your most sincere friends, and very obedient servants."

(Signed &c., by all.)

"The above is a true copy.

"J. HILL."

J. Hill's Answer to the foregoing, dated Pitcairn's Island, October 4th, 1833.

"MY VERY DEAR FRIENDS,—The lively interest which, from the beginning, I have taken in your welfare is well known to our mutual friends in England. And thus, since my arrival here, on the 28th October, 1832, you know yourselves. I can only observe, at this moment, in answer to the request which you have deemed requisite thus to re-iterate, that is repeat, in your joint letter to me of the 3rd instant, which you handed to me at our prayer-meeting yesterday, P.M., in reference to my continuing a while longer with you, &c., I would say that, notwithstanding the importance of time, I shall not, with the blessed Lord's will, think of leaving you until hearing from home, *i. e.* from the British Government, nor until my presence becomes no longer necessary in furtherance of the established welfare of your commonwealth and beloved little island. Being always,

"My friends, really and faithfully,
"Your well-wisher,
'(Signed) JOSHUA HILL.
"*Teacher, &c.*"

Extract from a Note from Edward Quintal, one of the principal Elders, dated Pitcairn's Island, 6th April, 1833, to the Rev. George Pritchard, Missionary, Tahiti.

"OUR good friend, Capt. Hill, has been, and is doing all in his power for our general welfare; and I am sure that his plans are well calculated to insure both our present and future happiness. He will, doubtless, write to you fully himself, to which I must beg thus to refer you for particulars. Being, Rev. Sir, your most faithful and obedient servant,

"(Signed) WILLIAM QUINTAL,
"for my father, EDWARD QUINTAL."

Copy of a Letter, dated 8th March, 1834, from the same to the same.

"REV. AND DEAR SIR.—I wish to avail myself of the

pleasure of transmitting you a line, for I have not time to say more at present, in regard to the very unpleasant state of things for a long while on our island; and I must observe to you *again* that, but for the presence of Capt. Hill, we never could have been able to have got on, against the exceeding bad proceedings of the three foreigners among us. But now, the Lord be ever praised! the whole cause being removed, we have no doubt whatever, the effect will be immediate union among the natives." [This letter was sent by the vessel which took the three exiles hence to Tahiti, April 8th, 1834.] "Capt. Hill has all along acted like a father to us all, and we really owe him more than we shall ever be able to discharge. I cannot conceive how any person could have attempted to stigmatize, by the frigate *Challenger*, a gentleman of his just pretensions; but Capt. Freemantle soon saw through the intention and design, &c. Hoping you are all well, I am, Rev. and dear Sir, your most obedient servant,

"(Signed) for my father, EDWARD QUINTAL,

"WILLIAM QUINTAL."

Copy of a Note from Capt. C. H. Freemantle, R.N., dated, Challenger, *off Pitcairn's Island, Jan. 12th, 1833, to Joshua Hill, Pitcairn's Island.*

"MY DEAR SIR,—I have the pleasure to return the papers you were good enough to allow me to have to copy." [These papers were merely in regard to the island; next, Capt. F. speaks of some articles which he was so kind as to send me, and finishes by observing that] "I shall always be glad to hear of the welfare of the inhabitants of Pitcairn's Island, and I most sincerely trust that they will continue to go on and prosper, be happy, and contented. I shall exert myself on my arrival in England in furthering your views with respect to a clergyman being sent to them, which, I think, may be accomplished.* A letter addressed to, &c.

"Wishing you every happiness, I am, my dear Sir, yours faithfully,

"(Signed)   CHAS. H. FREEMANTLE."

Copy of a Note from Professor Alex. Mackinnon to J. Hill.

"MY DEAR SIR,—Mrs. Mackinnon has settled with the doctor to innoculate our little girl with the *vaccine pus* this evening about five o'clock; this, of course, deprives her and myself of the pleasure which we, as well as every other person, must always enjoy in your agreeable and interesting company. Discourses on subjects so great and sublime as occupied the talents and goodness of a Newton, a Boyle, a Bacon, and a D'Alembert, and to which you pay such attention, must interest and improve the mind of every rational person and admirer of the great and wonderful Author of the world, and all the phenomena that surround them.

"We both trust, in a few days, to have the pleasure of taking tea with you."

* "The clergyman to succeed in my duties, &c."

"Pitcairn's Island, 20th June, 1834.

"MY LORD,—I have the honour to address your Lordship, in consequence of the people here petitioning your Excellency's protection, in relation to certain evil designs which immediately concern their interest and welfare upon this island. I take leave, in the first instance, to state to your Lordship that whilst at home, in the years 1828 and 1829, during the Duke of Wellington's administration, some letters passed between His Majesty's Government and myself, with respect to the transferring of these people hence to Tahiti. This was about the time, or a little after, of Capt. Beechy's (R. N. of H. M. S. *Blossom*) return home from the Pacific. My affairs, however, and then indifferent state of health, kept me in England till June 1830, when I embarked, as a passenger, for the coast of Chili and Peru, where my stay was but transient; then to the Sandwich Islands. I remained between three and four months; and, in the interval, at the special request of the Government and Missionaries, I assisted them, so far as was in my power, in furtherance of the general good. I next embarked for the Society Islands, and continued, or rather, I should say, was again detained nearly a year there, at the most particular desire of the Missionaries and the Government (as their letters also to me can show). I devoted a good deal of my leisure time as well, in furtherance of their mutual interest. A little before I left Tahiti, however, there arose, unfortunately, certain differences, as to mere opinion, between the Rev. gentlemen and myself. The first was in relation to the deleterious and ungentlemanly habit of making (too free) use of strong drink at Tahiti, to the immediate prejudice of those with whom they had, and must have, to do—example being everything. Thus, they were pleased to consult me on certain points, and I freely and candidly gave them my humble opinion. They knew from me, from the moment I arrived among them, that I was merely a private individual, visiting the islands for my health, and, as a sincere friend to the Missionary cause, to render my little aid, which by any possibility my poor abilities might afford—the more especially respecting shipping, nautical affairs, certain laws, &c. But upon my begging them (the Rev. gentlemen) to establish at once a temperance society (which, alas! they then had no mind to do) at Tahiti—although it seems they have since been compelled, *i. e.* with regard to ardent spirits only—not wine—(was I merely to get a little inebriated on wine, I could not blame my sailors if they got drunk on rum!)—in consequence of directions from their society (the London Missionary) at home, upon the recent arrival out of the new Missionaries, by the *Tuscan,* whaler, which vessel touched here on her way to Tahiti, with them on board, and who spent a short time with me on shore. They did not relish the antidote.

"There were, besides, certain incongruities going on at Tahiti, in which I could not agree, by any means, with some of the Rev. gentlemen upon that station. And, as I had my information from themselves, and not picked up along shore, I can have no doubt on the matter. I could no longer suffer myself to be mystified, as, alas! is too usual, in regard to the real state of morals, &c., there; the more especially when a ship of note arrives among them, for a few days only. I allude to certain grave matters, hence must stop, lest I show a spirit of recrimination, which it becomes me to limit. But their conduct (the Missionaries') towards me here, however I regret upon their account and the cause which I am bound to respect, nay reverence, that is, the blessed work of the gospel, or be a mere nominal Christian,—actually compels me to break silence, when they sent word recently through a Capt. Henry to the people left under my charge here by Capt. Freemantle, that they would write your Lordship to have me removed 'dead or alive' (was the expression) from the island, and that their 'dear and affectionate friend,' George Nobbs, should be, with the other exiles, allowed to return, as before, here. This same Capt. Henry, whilst recently here, acknowledged to me, that he was perfectly aware that these foreigners were the principal, if not the whole, cause of the troubles at all the islands. I have told these people, over and over again, that they have only to behave themselves, and strictly to obey the orders of the British Government, or, which is the same, that of a captain of the British Royal Navy. But they are so easily alarmed and led away by the evil disposed, that I have considerable trouble to convince them of their real interest and duty. I promised Capt. Freemantle that I would remain in charge of these people till I could hear from His Majesty's Government on the subject, by which I have not yet been honoured by a word.

"And, since Capt. Freemantle left here, Mr. Nobbs has been doing us all the harm in his power, till he was shipped off hence the 8th March, 1834. I beg to assure your Lordship, that I have had much anxiety and trouble since I have been upon this island. These three men, exiled hence, have constantly been trying, by every means in their power, to degrade the church, to corrupt the school, as well as the people generally, and to lower me as their teacher, &c. They have even attempted to break in upon me in the middle of the night; but, my being armed and hearing them,—they escaped in the dark.

"I really could not think of leaving them thus situated, and agreed to do what I could for them, until I could hear from home, and receive the pleasure of His Majesty's Government. Capt. Freemantle arrived about two months after, and was pleased with what I had done. He sentenced these three men (three runaway common English sailors) to leave the island as early as possible; but, unfortunately for us, Capt. F. forgot to leave a line in regard to his orders. I beg now to solicit that your Excellency will be pleased to take the case of these people of Pitcairn's into consideration, and to address them a line of consolation, with respect to your Lordship's commands, for their future government, against the illegal proceedings of those persons sent here from Tahiti, to disturb the peace, tranquillity, and good order (otherwise) of the island.

"As for myself, my Lord, I have now no greater wish or desire than to spend the little time which may yet be allowed me, by a gracious Lord and Master, in furtherance of his cause, and in preparing, in the best way I can, for a life to come.

"I am now becoming infirm, being in the sixty-second year of my age, and, of course, must go hence ere long.

"Through the salubrity of this climate, notwithstanding all that I have to do in my several duties, besides vexations from evil-disposed persons, my general health has been far better than I could have expected. I pray your Lordship will be pleased also to allow me to make reference, in other respects, to the accompanying papers, the more especially to the petition itself of the people, as to since I have been with them; and to pardon this hastily written letter.

"I have the honour to be, my Lord, your Lordship's most obedient humble servant,

"(Signed) J. HILL.

'Lord James Townshend,
"British Commander in Chief, &c., &c., &c.,
"Upon the West Coast of South America."

"Pitcairn's Island, June 22nd, 1834.

"MY LORD,—I beg to avail myself of an extra moment allowed me, since writing the accompanying hasty letter to your Lordship, to say that the actual population of this island is about sixty-two souls. They are fast increasing, and the major part are young persons and children. I have about forty scholars on my school list, between the age of four and seventeen years. The

island is well supplied with the most essential articles; water being (*per se*) one main exception, which it becomes requisite to manage. Pitcairn's is remarkably healthy; wood plenty; the finest yams, potatoes (*Convolvulus batata*), and plantains; hogs, fowls, ducks, and fish; a young cow and bull; three donkeys. And in furtherance of the plan I suggested to my friends in England (be pleased to see paper No. 4), with regard to these people, is to instruct them, as far as may be possible for their general welfare, according to right reason and sound doctrine; and, especially, in ethics, industry, the mechanical arts; and to keep under the growing population by encouraging emigration—thus going forth from time to time as native teachers to the other islands, as in another generation the population here must in due course become very dense for so small an island, of about five miles in circumference, and a considerable part mountain land. They should begin in time to cultivate as well domestic economy.*
I wish, moreover, to instruct them in the essential art of governing themselves hereafter, and in state policy. A present they are too much like children, and have scarcely been taught anything (old John Adams himself, a common sailor, was very limited) thus for their good. In 1825, Capt. Beechy informs us, that he found them at prayer from morning till night, whereas I found them, in 1832, more fond of play than prayer or work,—a little of each would perhaps be best. I have the honour

---

* "There has been a great relief to the isle, in the recent removal of the three exiles with their families (to Gambier's or Lord Hood's), eighteen persons in number."

to be, my Lord, your Lordship's most obedient humble servant.

" (Signed)   J. Hill.

"To Lord James Townshend.

" In the event of your Lordship having occasion to send a ship of war this way, may I beg that the captain may receive instructions to look over my documents and private papers, which I happen to have here with me, and report the same to your Lordship.

"J. Hill."

" The Humble Petition of the Principal Native Inhabitants of Pitcairn's Island, dated 19th June, 1834, to His Excellency Lord James Townshend, Commander in Chief of His Britannic Majesty's Naval Forces upon the west coast of South America, &c. &c. &c.

" Sir,—We, the undersigned public functionaries of Pitcairn's Island, humbly beg leave to address your Lordship, and thus implore, that your Lordship will be pleased to have pity on us, and take cognizance of our truly unfortunate case. Your Lordship will, in the first place, be pleased to understand, that ever since the death of old Mr. John Adams (*i. e.* Alexander Smith, of H. B. M. S. *Bounty*), now about five years, we have been divided in party spirit, through the presence alone of three worthless fellows (runaway English sailors, whom, alas! we allowed to stop on the island), by the names of John Buffett, George Nobbs, and John Evans. At times we have had two schools and two churches, whilst at other times we have had neither the one nor the other, and at best very deficient, as may naturally be supposed; until the month of October, 1832, when Mr. Joshua Hill, an English gentleman (our actual teacher and pastor), providentially, as we conceive, arrived here in the barque *Pomare* from Tahiti, where, it would seem, he had been doing them all the good in his power, as it seems he had previously done at the Sandwich Islands. Mr. Hill brought us a very strong letter of introduction from our friends (as we were then willing and happy to consider the Reverend gentlemen), the Missionaries at the beautiful Tahiti; though, alas! unrestrained people. And ever since Mr. Hill's arrival, more than a year and a half, we have, the Lord be praised! had a regular school, and the Church of England service twice every Sabbath, with a lecture on some good subject. Besides, Mr. Hill established at once a Temperance Society (which we very much needed), and our present government, such as it is, of elders, sub-elders, and cadets; as well as prayer meetings and various other necessary things for our good, in which he is constantly employed; and who has throughout, and in all respects, acted towards us all as a real father. We have recently improved considerably our bad landing-place, the road to the village, &c.; but lamentable to state, whilst thus occupied for the general interest and welfare of our little commonwealth, these three licentious men were putting every difficulty and impediment in the way that they could possibly invent or forge by false reports, slanders, or misleading and corrupting the more ignorant of the people. Capt. Freemantle, R.N., of H. B. M. S. *Challenger*, whilst here, a little after Mr. Hill's arrival, did, it is true, judge and sentence them to leave the island, that is, Buffett and Nobbs (and Evans we have also been obliged since to condemn); but, unfortunately for us, Capt. Freemantle forgot and omitted, after going on board the frigate, in the hurry of sailing in the evening, to send as we expected a memorandum, or written paper, of what he had done, agreeable to his promise. He was highly satisfied that Mr. Hill had agreed to sacrifice his time here for our interest, till he could hear from home, and receive answers from the British Government on the subject, which he has not yet been honoured with. Capt. Freemantle, moreover, promised on his arrival at home, to use his influence in procuring a proper person to succeed Mr. Hill. On the 8th March, an English whaler (the *Tuscan* of London) arrived, and we succeeded with the master to take the three said exiles off, and he would have taken their families as well had they wished him, but they had no desire then to take them. Hence, they proceeded direct to Tahiti, and there, it appears, represented to the Missionaries the greatest falsehoods; and which, strange to conceive, were believed or regarded by them, notwithstanding they had been made duly acquainted with the facts by us (as an act of mere courtesy on our part to the Reverend gentlemen), that these three troublesome men had been sent off and exiled for ever from the island. But, however, on the 11th June, 1834, the barque *Pomare*, Ebril, master, of and from Tahiti, arrived off here with our three said exiles on board, and they (the master Ebril and his brother-in-law, a Capt. Henry, the son and son-in-law of one of the Missionaries of Tahiti) represented to us, that they were charged by the Missionaries of Tahiti, to place George Nobbs (one of our exiles) either here again or at Gambier's Isle, as a colleague and Missionary from them. We told them that these men had been banished the island by Capt. Freemantle and ourselves, and hence we could not upon any account whatever allow either of them to land; when Henry hastily remarked, 'Who is Capt. Freemantle?' (recovering himself a little, continued) 'he's but a mere man!' This Capt. Henry wished to make us believe, that he had also received a commission from the British Government, to come here and settle all our difficulties, as a regular-appointed consul for the islands in the Pacific. But upon our venerable teacher begging him to favour us with a sight of said credentials, as it regarded Pitcairn's, we heard no more about his consulship. They then determined on taking off the three exiles again, together with their families and all their things. They also took with them three other persons, whom they corrupted to accompany them to Hood's Island, as they pretended, to settle there; but in truth, we think they have certain designs hereafter, with respect to our island again. They further represent, that 'there was at Tahiti an American brig with fifty-five men on board, about coming to destroy Pitcairn's,' for sending off these three men. Your Lordship will, perhaps, scarcely credit that this Capt.

Henry (the son of a Tahitian Missionary, an Irishman), during the two days here, tried all he could to corrupt our women, both married and single, he being a married man himself. He actually took away with him one of our men, George Adams, who has left behind his wife and three children, under a promise, it is said, that the Missionaries at Tahiti would send him home, and recommend him to the British Government; which, it is added, would be sufficient for the appointing him, George Adams, governor of Pitcairn's Island. That then he would send off our old teacher (meaning our present respected and aged pastor), and recal the exiles from Hood's Island, was the inference. Moreover, George Nobbs, beyond a doubt, with a man named Bunker (the master, Nobbs being his mate), ran away with the latter vessel or boat, in which they two alone came here, about five years ago, from the Spanish coast; and we have received four different accounts, that their boat's crew was actually made away with before they set out. In case your Lordship should wish to know the truth of this affair, your Lordship would only have to give directions to the Spanish public authorities on the coast, to make the necessary inquiries touching the subject. The little vessel in which the master (Bunker) and the mate (Nobbs) came here about five years ago, entirely alone, had been employed in the sealing trade, among the little islands on the coast; and they themselves said that at the port of Guayaquil they fitted out, but their accounts thus are not to be depended upon. It is said that there were five or six men (their little crew) made away with. Bunker committed suicide, and Nobbs destroyed his papers. The vessel was broken up here, and unfortunately, from that time Nobbs became our teacher in opposition to Buffett, who already was bad enough. It may not perhaps be amiss to acquaint your Lordship further, that another main object of these three lazy men has been to get and obtain for their children as much of our land from us as possible. But Mr. Hill having opened our eyes thus, Capt. Freemantle at once decreed, that no one, otherwise than a native born, was to hold or possess any land whatever upon the island. For, as their families augmented in number, and it was pretty fast (fourteen children between the three exiles), they must have more land or give up keeping school. What could we do? but to work their ground besides, and their women labour hard, whilst themselves would scarcely do more than to overlook, 'eat, drink, and be merry.'

"Your Lordship's petitioners most humbly beseech and entreat your Lordship's benevolence, thus protecting us all here under the British flag, as loyal subjects. And that your Lordship will be pleased, as early as may be possibly convenient, to honour and forward to us a letter of instructions as to how we should act and conduct ourselves aright, which is, and ever shall be our main object. We wish to follow the orders of the British Government only, or, which is the same, that of a Captain in the British Royal Navy. We beg now to offer the assurance of unfeigned deference and respect with which we have the honour to be your Lordship's most faithful and obedient humble servants.

"(Signed)   Arthur $\overset{his}{\underset{mark.}{\times}}$ Quintal,

"William $\overset{his}{\underset{mark.}{\times}}$ Young,

"Edward $\overset{his}{\underset{mark.}{\times}}$ Quintal,

"John Quintal,

"Elders.

"Fletcher Christian,

"William $\overset{his}{\underset{mark.}{\times}}$ M'Coy,

"Sub-elders.

"Arthur Quintal,
"William Quintal,
"Matthew Quintal,
"Charles Christian, Jun.

"Cadets."

"We the undersigned certify that the foregoing is a true copy from the original, written by me,

"William Quintal.

"This the said copy being written by me,

"Arthur Quintal, Jun.

"Done at the express orders of all the public functionaries on Pitcairn's Island.

"Arthur Quintal, Jun.,
"William Quintal,

"Cadets."

[Copy.]

"I AM aware that pedantry and egotism become no one, and myself perhaps less than any. (Pro. xxvii. 2.) But for certain reasons, the following credentials, as a memorandum, I hope will be pardoned on the present occasion—they are truths.

"I observe, *in limine*, that I have visited the four quarters of the globe, and it has ever been my desire to maintain, as far as lay in my power, the standing of an English gentleman. I have lived a considerable while in a palace, and had my dinner parties with a princess on my right, and a General's lady upon my left. I have had a French cook, a box at the Opera. I have drove my dress carriage (thought the neatest then in Paris, where I spent five or six years; as well I have known Calcutta), and the handsomest lady (said), Madame R——, to grace my carriage. I have drove a curricle with my two outriders, and two saddle-horses, besides a travelling-carriage. A valet, coachman, footman, groom, and, upon extraordinary occasions, my *maître d'hôtel*. I have (at her request) visited Madame Bonaparte, at the Tuileries, St. Cloud, and Malmaison. I might thus mention many others of note abroad. I have frequently dined with that remarkable woman, Madame Carburas, afterwards the Princess de C——. I have had the honour of being in company, *i.e.* at the same parties, with both his late Majesty George IV. then Prince Regent, and his present Majesty William IV. then H. R. H. Duke of Clarence, as well with their royal brothers. I have ridden in a royal Duke's carriage, with four horses and three footmen, more than once, and have dined at his table, and drunk the old hock of his late father George III. I have visited and dined with some of our first families, and have been visited by a Duke, and others of the first noblemen. I have known and dined with (abroad and in England) Madames Catalini, Grassini, Georges, &c. And I have given the arm to Lady Hamilton (of Naples renown), whom the hero of the Nile has given his (one) to more than once. I have dined with a viceroy Governor (who was a General and a Count), and with Admirals, both on board their ships and on shore. I have entertained Governors, Generals, Captains (R. N.), on board my ship, more than once. And I have commanded several ships, and went to sea at the beginning of the French Revolution. I have been acquainted with many military and naval officers. I have since 1807, my admittance, from the late President, Sir Joseph Banks, to the sittings of the Royal Society. I have occasionally breakfasted with Sir Joseph, and visited, and even presented a friend (the actual President of the bank of the N. N. S. of America) to his evening parties. My admittance to the Royal Society has always admitted me to similar institutions abroad. I received the dress sword, and nautical instruments, &c. of a noble lord (at his death), a Vice-Admiral of the Red. I sailed from England (Portsmouth, May 1st, 1794) to the East Indies and China, in the largest fleet, possibly, that ever was; it was under Lord Howe, down the British Channel, just one month before his great victory. I have visited the Falls of Niagara and Montmorency, the natural bridge in Virginia, the great Reciprocating Fountain in East Tennessee, the great Temple of Elephanta at Bombay. I have dined with a prince, as well as with a princess; and with a count, a baron, an ambassador, a minister (ordinary and extraordinary), and have travelled with one for some weeks. I have dined with a *Chargé d'Affaire*, and lived with consuls, &c. I have visited and conversed with 'Red Jacket,' the great Indian warrior. I have visited and been visited by a bishop. I have frequently partook of the delicious Hungarian wine (*tokey*), Prince Easterhazy's; as also of Prince Swantzerburgh's old hock, said to have been 73 years old; and I was intimate with the brother-in-law of this last German nobleman. I have dined with a principal Hong merchant at Canton. I have sat next to the beautiful Madame Recamier and Madame Carbanus, at the great dinner parties. I have written to the Prime Minister of England; and have received the (late Earl of Liverpool's) answer with his thanks, &c. I was at Paris when the allies were made there. I have visited and breakfasted with the late Warren Hastings, Esq., at his seat in Gloucestershire. I have had permission with a party of friends to hunt over his grounds. Entertained &c. two or three days at the sporting lodge of an Earl, now a Marquis. I have made a crimson silk net for a certain fashionable Marchioness, which she actually wore at her next great party of five or six hundred persons. I have danced with the

Countess Bertand, *i. e.* Mademoiselle Fanny Dillon, before she married the Marshall. I was at Napoleon's coronation. I have been invited to the Lord Mayor's, and to the dinner of an Alderman of London ; to those also of the first merchants and bankers, as the late Mr. Thelusson (afterwards Lord Rendlesham), the formerly rich Messrs. A. and B. Goldsmiths, &c. And at Paris I have had a credit of 400,000 francs, at one time, on the house of Perregan, Lafitte, &c., and other bankers at Paris for considerable sums. Delepent and Co. for 40,000 francs, and Recamier's, at one time, for upwards of 100,000 francs. Lafitte's house at another time for 50,000 francs ; again for 12,000 francs. I have had at a time, nearly £5000 sterling at the Bank of England. I wrote and published in the London *Morning Post* (7th March, 1811), on naval power. I have seen the Vestrises, father, son, and grandson, at once (the only time), dance on the stage at the opera at Paris. I have given a passage to many on board my ship, but never in my life received a farthing as passage-money from any person. I am decidedly against the use of ardent spirit (malt liquor may do for those who like it), tobacco, &c. And as for wine, that only at dinner ; it even then ought to be good, if not the very best, as the *Gourmet* would have it, when speaking of Clas-Vangeat, and Romance, &c. I have had a fine band of music on board my ship, and my four kinds of wine on my table. (I am not sleeping on a 'bed of roses' now, but in an humble hut or cabin.) After all, what does the foregoing amount to ?—vanity of vanities. I will merely add, that I have had a year in the Church of Christ, and that I am a life member of the Bible Society. That I am looking with the blessed Lord's help to something of far more intrinsic worth and consideration—'the price of our high calling'—the life to come. I am now in my sixty-second year of age, and of course it is high time that I should look upon this world as nearly to close on me. I might perhaps say much more, but must stop.* I am now an humble teacher upon Pitcairn's Isle for the time being.

"June, 1834.

"(Signed)   J. HILL.

"Touching J. Hill's, &c.,
"June, 1834."

[Copy.]
"H. M. S. *Blonde*, Callao,
"Jan. 2nd, 1836

"SIR,—I had the honour to receive, on the 28th ult., your letter of the 3rd October, 1835, enclosing copies of letters from the Secretary of the Admiralty and Mr. Hay, with other documents relative to the Pitcairn islanders, and desiring me to go or send a vessel there, to investigate the conduct of Mr. Hill, and to unde-

---

* "I have had a Member of Parliament, an East India Director, call on me to ask a favour which, indeed, no one else could grant. I have his note thus still. And I have had a beautiful Egyptian lady write to me (I have her note also still), the wife of one of Bonaparte's Generals."

ceive the people as to his authority, &c. In reply, I beg to inform you, that I have always felt a very strong interest for that most exemplary and Christian Society, and that nothing but the revolutionary state of Peru, since February last, and a foreign war since June, which has put the persons and property of His Majesty's subjects, in common with other foreign merchants, to great hazard, together with the loss of the *Challenger*, has prevented my going or sending; but in consequence of various letters which I received, as far back as Dec. 1834, I wrote at various times to the victims of Mr. Hill's tyranny and oppression, and to Mr. Pritchard at Tahiti, informing them of my firm conviction that he had no right to assume any authority on the island, much less to use corporal punishment, or to send any of the inhabitants away. I will, however, take the earliest opportunity of going, or sending a vessel, there, and hope to hear that the letters I wrote produced the effect I wished, of releasing the inhabitants from Mr. Hill's tyranny and oppression, and of restoring to the island those whom he had driven away.

"I have the honour to be, Sir,
"Your obedient Servant,
"(Signed)   FRANCIS MASON, &c. &c. &c.
"*Commander.*"

IN concluding my labour of love, and, while commending my little book to the good wishes of my readers, I would still wish to say one word more as to the future prospects of Pitcairn's Island, which forms its theme. The nucleus of a committee has already been formed, for the purpose of benefiting its simple inhabitants, by supplying them with clothing and many other necessary articles, which they much require: and, it is to be hoped, that those who feel an interest in the subject of the aforesaid pages, will apply either to John Shillinglaw, Esq., of 14, Chatham-place, Blackfriars, who has kindly consented to act as Honorary Secretary; or to myself, who will be most happy to afford any information on the subject.

In conclusion, I have no doubt that many of my own friends would like to know what became of myself after leaving Pitcairn's Island, and also of my old ship the *Noble*, which left me behind. After leaving Pitcairn's Island, on the 13th of April, 1850, I sailed in the barque *Colonist*, bound to San Francisco. I must say that my berth on board her was not the most pleasant; nor could I expect to be made more comfortable, going on board in the manner in which I did, as there really was no spare room for an extra passenger, the *Colonist* being a small vessel with 144 passengers (miners), besides a crew of forty men. Bad as my situation was, I felt quite contented, as it was probably my only chance, for many months, of getting away. Everything on board was conducted in the most disorderly manner. The captain was a kind-hearted man, and had no control over any of the passengers. The consequence was, that the conduct and language of nearly every one on board cannot be described; and as for the diet, the less I say upon this matter the better. My bed was upon the spare leaf of the mess-table, it being too large for the cabin; with the loan of a blanket from one, a rug from another, and a sail for a pillow, I managed pretty well, or as comfortably as circumstances would permit.

April 20*th.* The weather now became very cold, and I felt much, not having sufficient warm clothing of my own; and no one was inclined to lend to me, although their promises were so liberal before going on board at Pitcairn's Island. Times were bad, but then I was going to California; my hardships, therefore, did not appear so intolerable as they really were, as at the same time, I knew I had seen worse days than these in my previous travels, having been twice round the world—in Russia, Prussia, Norway, Sweden, Denmark, France, The Cape Verd, Canary, and Western Islands or Azores, Bombay, Madras, Calcutta, Coast of Malaba, Penang, Malacca, Singapoore, Sumatra, Java, Canton, Macoa, Lintin, Cape of Good Hope, St. Helena, Ascension, Upper and Lower Canada, Lakes Superior, Ontario, and Erie; 1000 miles through the United States of America; Havannah, Panama, Acapulco, Australia, New Zealand, thirty-five islands in the South Seas, and last, not least, in California.

April 24*th.* Crossed the equator, and all hands performed the usual ceremony of doing Neptune honour; but in a very tame manner, not at all like what I had seen in former days, having crossed the equator no less than thirty-four different times. My messmates consisted of my friend Carleton, and four second-cabin passengers from Adelaide, all of whom were obliged to take it in turn weekly to cook for the mess.

May 5th. My turn for cooking arrived, which was anything but an agreeable task, more especially as it was among the most noisy passengers I ever met with. Cooking for a week among such a set of creatures as these, certainly broke one in for the hardships and treatment a Californian gold digger might expect. As to discipline there was none, and it was twelve o'clock at night before any rest could be obtained; and the only manner of getting sleep was to work hard in some way during the day, as the innumerable enemies below (I mean those little creatures that are magnified to many thousands of times their own size at the Polytechnic and other exhibitions in London) often caused a sleepless night.

May 28th. I arrived in San Francisco, after being six weeks upon short allowance of provisions and water, and much shorter of clothing. I often thought of the clothes I was promised when I first went on board: but the hearts of those around me were about on a par with the hearts of the real gold diggers. Upon landing, I found that the barque *Noble* had not arrived. At this horrid sink of iniquity I counted about 600 ships lying at anchor off the town, most of which were deserted by their crews, who had gone to the diggings to make a fortune, or leave their bones there. The latter often happened, but the former seldom; although we have heard so much through the public press of the immense gains that have been made in California.

May 29th. I went on shore with *all* my clothes under my arm, which was anything but a heavy load; and all the money I was possessed of was 4s., which I was pressed to take from one of the Pitcairn islanders, saying that I should not land in California without a sixpence. Four shillings in California, at that time, were about equal in value to *one* sixpence here. It went all at once to pay for one meal, and glad was I to get a good one, not thinking at the time that I was spending all I had. I met a man during the day that knew me in New Zealand, who offered me a part of his tent, whose offer I gladly accepted. There were nearly one hundred New Zealand people living in San Francisco that I knew, and many of whom were well off, yet not *one* of them offered me the value of a sixpence. Most of these people had risen from nothing, and the greater part of them had received many pounds from, and were under obligations to me, when in New Zealand. But, my friends, this is California. The first two days I was on shore I could not get anything to do; times here were not what they had been, although onions were now selling at 9s. per lb., and potatoes £120 per ton, and other luxuries in proportion. This day I borrowed fifteen dollars from two New Zealand colonists; on the third day I managed to obtain a few hours' employment at 4s. per hour. The next day I obtained employment with the same people, two Yankee gents, brothers. I lent one of them my manuscript of Pitcairn's Island to read, thinking it as well to let them know in an indirect manner what sort of person I was, what was my real position, and also my late misfortunes. Lending this journal was a good *hit* for me. Only fancy! after receiving 24s. for my day's work, my employer took me to his house, and we supped together; in fact, I had breakfast, dinner, and supper all in one meal, not an unfrequent occurrence with many deluded Californians. For several days I worked with my friend, the younger brother, and we soon became very intimate, he being a fresh hand from New York. I soon was my own master, and made many improvements about the premises, which otherwise would not have been thought of. These two brothers now began to think me very useful; and as I had made a few dollars, I began to feel rather independent. Having completed all they had for me to do, I left them; they promising to employ me whenever they needed any one. I was now in a situation to renew my wardrobe, which I took advantage of, at most expensive prices I must confess; such as, boots at £6 to £8 sterling per pair, &c. &c. After a few days, I engaged with four others to discharge a large Sydney ship at so much per ton; and the very first night I went on board, to take up my abode during the time of discharging, I lost all my new wardrobe overboard, through the carelessness of another person. I now, once more, had nothing left to trouble me excepting a few dollars, and those I should have lost, had I not kept a good look out after them. Two-thirds of the houses in San Francisco are gambling-houses and grog-shops; and the company, as you may suppose, not very select.

June 14*th*. The city of San Francisco was on fire. I was engaged blowing up houses with gunpowder, and undermining and pulling them down, to check the fire from spreading over the whole place, which burned with awful fury, the wind at the time blowing a complete gale. Saved much property, for which I was handsomely paid. This day, for a wonder in California, I, like many others, dined free of any expense; having dined off sardins and preserved meats, which had been partially baked in the fire, the owners of these meats telling us to eat what we liked, but not to take any away. Biscuits were strewed about in all directions, and tons of fine New Zealand potatoes, already cooked. During the whole day, wine and beer were given gratuitously from every house to any one who called for them. One million sterling of property was supposed to have been destroyed this day, but no lives lost; and many people who had been burned out, were actually on the same evening rebuilding their houses upon the same ground, before the fire was thoroughly extinguished. The fire-men and carpenters, in many places, were at work upon the same spot together.

June 25*th*. This day the long looked for barque *Noble* arrived, having been ninety-three days from Pitcairn's Island, the crew having suffered great privations from want of provisions and water. It happened to have been a most fortunate occurrence, my being left upon Pitcairn's Island. There I was well treated for sixteen days, and after all, arrived at San Francisco twenty-eight days before my old ship, the *Noble*. I considered it was a judgment upon the captain and supercargo, for their wickedness in leaving five of their passengers on the island, having had an excellent opportunity of taking us all off on the 28th March. In fact, nearly the whole of the crew went on the quarter-deck and remonstrated with the captain on that day, stating to him the cruel and unfeeling conduct he had displayed. My opinion, given on the 28th of March, was perfectly correct; they considering their onions and potatoes more valuable than those passengers that were left upon the island. But had they taken us on board again, which they could have done without losing one hour, they would have been compelled then to have gone into the Sandwich Islands for provisions and water, and have sold their whole cargo at a very handsome profit for their owners, for whom I am sorry; but it serves them right, for sending two such inefficient men in charge of their property. In place of making a profit, I am afraid the owners will loose some thousands of pounds sterling; so that, in fact, we were all five of us far more fortunate in being left upon the island, than those that deserted us. Had the United States laws been in operation in California, Capt. Parker would have been placed in an awkward position, as well as the little supercargo; as the whole of the ship's company, including the officers, were determined to state the real facts before the court, if they were called upon by me. The captain and supercargo tried, in every possible manner, to make the crew believe that there was no chance of taking us off. When I asked the captain why he did not attempt to take us off, he endeavoured to persuade me that he did not see the island; but when I told him what they were doing when they passed the island, and what particular sail they had set, he then made an excuse, and said, "The wind would not permit of it." I then asked for the log-book, when I was told by the mate that there was none on board. Fancy a ship without a log-book! Unfortunately, the captain died some two months after his arrival in California of cholera. I took all my clothes and everything I had out of the *Noble* on shore. I then went up the Sacramento river to the city of Sacramento, in a small vessel which I chartered, on a trading speculation, and visited the cities of New York, Benecia, and Stockton. The former consisted of eleven houses —six were eating-houses and grog-shops, three were empty, one baker, and one butcher. I afterwards went to San José, where, on the 28th of October, I was seized with the cholera; but fortunately knowing the symptoms (having had it once before), I used the necessary precautions in time, which, in all probability, saved my life. I was then in the Guadalope River, at Alviso (the embarkadero of San José), on board of a small coasting vessel, alone, the captain being absent on business. Fortunately, I soon found a medical man, who gave me half a tumbler of brandy, laudanum, and camphor, with orders to go on board the vessel and go to bed, cover myself with blankets, and, if possible, get into a great perspiration, which luckily took place. The vessel being aground on the steep bank of the river at low water, and not being properly attended to, in the middle of the night she capsized over into the river, and nearly filled with water. This was rather an awkward position for a man to be in, with cholera upon him, and no one to help him. Here I was, in the middle of the night, compelled to turn out of a hot bed, in a most profuse perspiration, amidst a very cold and mizzling rain, to seek another abode for the night. The vessel being capsized, I got upon her bottom as well as I could, with two large blankets round me. I was then obliged to jump from the vessel on to the bank of the river, knee deep into a dark, soft mud, the only means I had of getting on shore. I then had to walk some distance in this state before I could find the doctor's house, which was only half built, but the best accommodation in the place; here I made my bed on the bare boards of the floor, there being no spare ones in the house. A fire was lighted, and, with my two blankets, I soon made myself as comfortable as circumstances would admit of, and slept sound for many hours. My doctor (Whitmore) was a good, honest, man, who told me he lived to cure patients, not to make money by them—an exception to the general rule among Californian medical men. I went into the interior, for change of air, for a few days, and then was recommended to leave the country immediately, as the only means of saving my life.

Nov. 12th. I left San Francisco in the *Antelope* steamer for Panama, with four hundred passengers, and arrived at the latter place on the 4th of December. This steamer was on fire five times during this voyage. At one time I thought nothing could have saved us. The different fires occurred from sheer negligence alone. Our provisions on board were of the worst description, and on the smallest scale of allowance—not the fault of the captain, but of the agent at San Francisco (Oliver Charlic). Parties arriving at Panama, either from the Pacific or Atlantic side, are liable to be greatly imposed upon; those from the Pacific less so than from the Atlantic, as their eyes have been well opened in California, in witnessing every description of roguery. After remaining here for twenty hours, as there was not much to see, I left for Chagres. I walked across the isthmus, along with two hundred of my fellow-passengers, a distance of about twenty-five miles, which took two days to accomplish. We paid twenty-five dollars for each mule to carry our baggage across the isthmus. Many of my fellow-travellers lost their baggage by the roguery of the mule drivers. I should myself have been one of the unfortunate ones, had I not taken the advice of a friend—which I recommend every traveller to follow—which is, to take the mule-master (*not the driver*) before the alcaldi or magistrate, paying for the mule or mules in the alcaldi's presence, and binding the mule-master down, in writing, to deliver your baggage safe at your journey's end; and if you find anything missing, you have only to produce your written agreement to the alcaldi, at your destination, who will see everything righted. On account of the heavy rain during the day, we were compelled to halt about eleven miles from Panama, neither the mules nor ourselves being able to get on, from the dreadful state of the road, which, in many places, was from two to three feet deep in mud. We put up for the night at what was called the American Hotel, half way between Panama and Cruces. This hotel was one large, long hut, without any flooring—a horrid hole—kept by a true-bred Californian gold-digger, a good specimen of the worst character. Three hundred and fifty of us slept in this *hotel*, some in hammocks, some in bunks, and the remainder—the largest number—on the ground in their wet clothes, few of them taking the trouble to change. Five shillings were charged for sleeping on the ground. I took the precaution, when I arrived here, to remove the bullocks' hides off my mules (which were placed there to keep the rain from my baggage), and reserve them to sleep upon, which, along with my blankets, made me up a very tolerable bed. My mule-driver and I had a great dispute about these bullocks' hides, as he wanted them for the same purpose as myself; ultimately I convinced him that I was entitled to them, having hired them at the same time that I hired the mules. About a mile further on the road, we heard that there was another sort of hotel for travellers, and that the party who kept it had (on the same night that we slept at the half-way house) burned opium, with the intention of sending every one of the travellers to sleep, with the hopes of robbing them of their gold dust. Fortunately it was discovered, and four men kept watch in turns during the whole night, much to the annoyance of the landlord and his wife (Americans). The next day I arrived at Cruces, which is a Mexican and Spanish settlement, nearly at the head of the Chagres river. The only hotel here was crowded with gold-diggers, homeward bound. There were many Mexicans and Spaniards who opened a sort of eating-house, and at night let their houses for parties to sleep in. Five friends and myself hired a house for the night, from a Mexican, for 12*s.*; but, previously to retiring to rest, we agreed that, in case an attack was made in the night (an occurrence not at all unusual among the Spaniards and Mexicans), to rob us of the gold dust we might have concealed about us, that we should jump into one particular corner of the room, so that we might not shoot each other in the dark, which was a very necessary precaution. However, nothing occurred during the night, perhaps on account of there being about 1000 Californians in the place—a number much above the native population. The road from Panama (twenty-five miles) was one of the most tedious roads I ever travelled. Some 150 years ago it was paved with large round stones by the Spaniards, to facilitate the carriage of heavy guns and treasure across the isthmus; these stones now were all displaced, and, for nearly half the distance, I could not walk upon *terra firma*, but had to step from stone to stone, which made it not only tedious but dangerous. Every now and then a mule would fall down into a mud hole, perhaps three or four feet deep; it was consequently obliged to be unloaded, which prevented the whole train from going on, it being unsafe to be left alone on this road, on account of the mountaineers.

The next day, *Dec. 7th,* twenty-seven of my fellow-travellers joined me, and we hired a boat to go down the river (Chagres) to Chagres, for which we paid £60, 15*s.,* or nine dollars (36*s.*) each, for taking us sixty miles down the river, with a strong current in our favour. Thus Californian prices appeared to follow the gold-digger even to his own home. On our way down the river, which was exceedingly picturesque, we passed four dead bodies (Americans), who had been lately drowned by the upsetting of a canoe, some say by the natives, who are in the habit of doing so, should they think there is much gold dust in the canoe, as they (the natives) can swim on shore; but the parties having much gold dust about them generally sink, as was the case with these poor fellows. Two of them, it is said, had as much as 10,000 dollars in dust round their bodies, which had been recently taken from them, by the marks on the bodies. We had nothing in our boat larger than a knife, or we should have picked them up and buried them. Such is the risk even in returning from California. This river abounds in alligators, turtle, guana, and fish. At night, just before dark, we arrived at Chagres, a most miserable-looking spot. Fortunately a large steamer took away 600 Californians this day for New York and New Orleans, or there would not have been any room for us in the town. For a small place, I consider it a more horrid spot than San Francisco. There were about forty or fifty houses, and, without one exception, every house was a hotel and grog-shop, and the people who kept them, judging from their appearance, likely to murder any one for a few dollars. We mustered about 1400 Californians here, the Spaniards and Mexicans all living on the opposite side of the river by themselves, which they preferred. It is about the most unhealthy place in Central America, on account of its low and swampy situation. During my stay here, which unfortunately was four or five days, an American gold-digger was detected in robbing another gold-digger of his bag of gold dust, amounting to 2000 dollars. He was tried by Lynch law, found guilty, and sentenced to twenty-four lashes across his back, and twenty-four drops of hot sealing-wax dropped upon his body, every two hours, until he confessed where it was. I must here remark, that there is a gang of what they call New Orleans Boys here, who are a party of about fifty of the worst description of pickpockets in the whole of the United States of America—some of them dressed in the most stylish manner, others quite the contrary, just to suit their several victims. These fellows go on board of every steamer from Chagres to the States that takes Californian diggers on board, in numbers varying from five to seven in company, according to the number of Californians. These parties go on board with the full determination of robbing every one they can of their gold dust, and very often succeed to a large amount. They generally manage, on the voyage between Chagres and New York or New Orleans, to find out who has, and who has not, gold dust concealed about them. Should they not have an opportunity of "plucking a good bird" (robbing a person before landing at his destination), these New Orleans light-fingered gentlemen have been known to follow people many hundred miles through the United States before they would give up their game.

Dec. 12*th.* I left Chagres for Havannah, in the steamer *Pacific,* of 1200 tons burthen. It is quite impossible to describe the shipping of 600 passengers on board of this vessel. In the first place, there was a heavy sea tumbling into the bay, which caused the steamer to roll about so fearfully, that, at times, the paddle-boxes were fifteen feet under water, and then, in a minute after, they were fifteen feet out of the water. There were then sixty-five boats full of passengers and their baggage, all trying to get on board at the same time, which made the undertaking of gaining the deck of the steamer most hazardous. The only accidents that happened were the smashing of two boats. When we all got on board, there was not room for every one to lie down at the same time. We were dreadfully crowded, but preferred being here rather than on shore at Chagres. Order or regulation was quite out of the question here. We got something to eat whenever we could; the provisions were very scanty, and irregularly supplied to the passengers; we were not allowed either knife or fork to eat our meals with; we were treated more like swine than human beings. On the fourth day after leaving Chagres we arrived at Havannah. I never shall forget the great contrast from barbarism in California to perhaps the most civilized and most highly polished society in the world. I went on shore to see the sights, in my rude Californian dress, which dress bore a great contrast to the elegantly dressed Spanish people. My dress, especially my boots, created some sensation on shore; and I can safely say, that I was never so much noticed in my life as the day I landed at Havannah. In every carriage that passed me—and they were very numerous, and generally filled with ladies—the first lady who observed my boots, was sure to give her companions notice of the approach of a Californian gold-digger, smiling either at me or my boots— an honour I had not had paid me for many long months. I visited the monument of Columbus, which was merely a marble bust, in the Cathedral, and whose ashes were brought from St. Domingo in 1822. The steamer *Pacific* being bound for New Orleans, I went on board the *Ohio* steam ship (a floating palace) of 2800 tons, bound for New York. Between eight and ten o'clock at night, by the light of the full moon, I walked about in the square opposite the Captain-General's palace, which was the promenade of the evening, and where the band was playing, and all the *élite* were enjoying themselves. The stylish dresses of some of the pretty Spanish ladies and the well-dressed gentlemen, made me believe that I had no business amongst them in such a dress—especially my boots. I at last got under a tree, near where the band was playing—shaded by the moon, so that I could see everything and everybody that passed without being much seen myself. Although in this secluded spot, every now and then a Spanish gentleman would come up to me, and ask permission to light his cigar from the fire in my little black pipe, which at times was issuing volumes of smoke; in fact, I did not see why I should not enjoy my little pipe, as the dandified gentlemen were enjoying their cigars. When the band left I left, and was proud to think that I had been a walking curiosity to the ladies during the day, and a benefit to the smoking gentleman during the night.

Dec. 18*th.* On Wednesday morning our steam was up, anchors weighed, and all the passengers, consisting of more than 300 in number, anxious to start for New York. Among them were some ladies from New Orleans and Havannah.

The steamer had proceeded a few yards on her way, when a violent jolt was felt over the whole vessel, as though striking against some heavy substance in the water. At once the engines were stopped, for an accident had occurred. Something had broken about the machinery, and, on examination, it proved to be the bursting of the cylinder-head of the starboard engine, which rendered it useless until repaired. It required several hours for the cooling of the water and metal, before the extent of the damage could be ascertained; but, when the exact state of affairs was known, it was pronounced impossible to repair the damaged engine before reaching New York. Only the larboard engine, therefore, was serviceable for the voyage. Captain Schenck, however, after mature consideration and reflection, determined to proceed to sea, although anticipating a longer passage, as one-half the power of the machinery was lost. He consequently made every preparation to meet the probable emergencies.

On Thursday, the 19th instant, we again weighed anchor, with some hopes and many forebodings. For the first two days our speed was good, but on the third it was somewhat diminished. As yet, no accident had occurred; the sea was tranquil, the sky serene, and no indications of a change. On Sunday evening, the wind freshened from the south-east, and before the next morning a tremendous storm blew from the north-west. It has never been my misfortune to witness at sea one of greater violence. The vessel reeled before the blast, and was tossed like a feather on the mountain waves.

At this time it was found impossible to proceed, as the engine stopped and the vessel "broached to." During Monday we lay to. But what a change had come over every object on board! As the storm rose, the steamer felt its effects; and with each successive roll articles were heard falling with a crash and noise unusual even in sailing vessels. The tables and chairs in the long dining saloon came together with a roar that left no doubt of their utter demolition. Now a crash followed, of glass and dishes; and jars and jellies, fruit and other delicacies, in the pantry, mingled their sweets with the general confusion. In the social hall, no better fate awaited its inmates. In the bar, kept for the accommodation of the passengers, the marble slab slid from its locality; the decanters, bottles, glasses, cordials, liquors, &c., started from their places; and the whole were strewn upon the floor in one common ruin. In the kitchen, a heavy bar had fallen upon the roof, crushing it in, through which the water poured. On deck the waves dashed their foam, and the spars were white with the saline spray, as if in a hoar frost.

When morning came, the scene was frightful to many, and gloomy to all. The fires between decks, except at the engine, were extinguished. Nothing warm to eat or to drink was to be had, for the kitchen was in water. No table could be used, for the pieces were upon the floor; and, withal, no dishes or other fragile ware remained. It was impossible to walk or even stand upon the deck, and equally impossible to sit elsewhere, without holding on to some fixture. For the most part, the passengers remained in their berths, but it was difficult to retain possession of them in the rolling of the vessel. In the saloon, the ladies, in terror and despair, had collected to receive whatever consolation and comfort the surrounding circumstances afforded. But with every lurch they were thrown from the sofas, or, if they clung to them, it was at the risk of a dislocated hand or arm. The gentlemen rendered them every assistance, although, at every change of locality they were liable (as happened often) to be tossed across the saloon, and retossed as the ship righted its position.

Cold meat, hard bread, and water, were all that could

be supplied from the stores on this sad Monday; and when the day closed, a more dismal sight of cheerless countenances has been seldom shut out from view where no positive disaster had occurred. Those who sought their state rooms to sleep, found it impossible to repose amid the roar of the waves without, the many sounds from within, and the violent lurching and tossing of the steamer; yet the wind had somewhat abated.

In the evening the engine had been put in motion, and we started on our course, but with little prospect of making much headway. Vessels had been seen during the day lying to, and some at short distances from us. One steamer had passed us to windward, bound apparently to Charleston, and with her steam up.

About midnight, the sad announcement was made from room to room that the vessel had sprung a leak, and was fast filling with water, that no time was to be lost, and every man on board was required at the pumps and buckets. It seemed as though we were about to perish, without even the mournful consolation of its being in the light of day. With a heavy but determined spirit, I put on the roughest of my clothing, ready to do my part to encounter the impending danger, and repaired on deck. I clung to the ropes and chains to save myself from falling overboard, while I looked around to penetrate the darkness of the hour. The engine had stopped, the fires were extinguished, and a thick mist, arising from the furnace, stifled my breathing. Here was an appaling sight; and what added to the catastrophe, was the fact that the pumps were all out of order, or in an unserviceable state. Some buckets were rigged, which were lowered down into the hold, and hand over hand the attempt was being made to discharge the water that was reported to be eleven feet in depth, and which had already risen to the level of the boilers. The efforts to start a pump ended in a failure, and our salvation depended upon four buckets which were in use. In the night, and in the rolling of the ship, the men clung to the ropes, and under every disadvantage the work of baling was going on.

After daylight, on Tuesday, a pump was put in order, and we began to make some impression on the leak. Again the "doctor" was able, with its pump, to throw out water; but the diminution of the quantity in the hold was not perceptible to many. During all this day all the passengers and hands worked faithfully at the pump and buckets. Yet everything was gloomy, uncomfortable, and desponding. At noon, however, the wind abated, and we hoped the sea would go down; still our exertions and our sufferings were the same. At night the leak was reached and stopped; but the general leakage, in the heavy roll of the sea, required unremitting attention. At this period, for the first time, the impression among the "knowing" (for we had four experienced captains on board) was that we were safe, unless a new misfortune should befall us. We were now nearly wearied out with constant labour and watching. Once in every three hours, for half an hour each time, all were called to the deck to labour in the wind, cold, and water. Wet and worn out, without rest, sleep, or warm food, we worked on, and Christmas morning dawned on the still cheerless scene.

Our efforts had now become perfectly regular and systematic. We knew every inch we had gained; the water had sunk to the level of the floor beneath the furnace, the fires were in a blaze, and we hoped we soon might have steam enough to help us. Unfortunately, the pump attached to the machinery was on the starboard engine, and consequently was useless. At last the engine was started, but a quantity of sheet iron had fallen near the shaft, and prevented its revolving. This impediment required time for its removal, and when done, it was discovered that coal had washed from the floor-grating below the crank. Here, again, hours were consumed. Fears also were entertained that even then the machinery would be crippled, and possibly unserviceable. About nine o'clock the coal was got out, and once more we started, and the vessel was steady. Now we could get comfortable, warm food to eat, which revived the drooping spirits and refreshed the strength of all. A tolerable dinner, at the proper time, was prepared, which was devoured with avidity.

At the request, in writing, of the passengers, our course was set for Norfolk, distant about 90 miles from our position. The work at the buckets and pumps still went on, and never ceased entirely until we anchored at Norfolk, State of Virginia.

In our dangers and difficulties the captain, his officers, and men, exhibited all the traits, skill, and energy of experienced seamen. Much praise was bestowed upon them, and too much cannot be awarded to them; but here my admiration for all that pertains to the *Ohio* must cease. Beyond the captain's department proper, there seemed to be a general neglect and mismanagement. The accident at Havannah might have been avoided if the steamer had been overhauled before starting to sea. She had been running constantly for 14 months, without finishing, without repairing, or coppering. She was unfit to encounter the dangers of the sea when leaving New Orleans.

The *Ohio* was on fire during the latter part of the gale, in the cook-house, on account of some fat falling into the fire, but only for a few minutes.

Dec. 26th. I left the *Ohio*, and went on board the steamer *Georgia*, of 600 tons, bound from here (Norfolk) to Baltimore; during the night the vessel caught fire, and burned with great rapidity. Fortunately, in about 35 minutes, it was got under by the crew. The captain being afraid to inform the passengers of their danger, in consequence of their being so many· on board (360), thinking that the confusion it would create would be worse than the fire, there were not more than six of us who knew anything about it until daylight the next morning. Landed at Baltimore on the 27th, and proceeded to New York *viâ* Philadelphia.

Jan. 4th, 1851. I left New York for Liverpool in the packet-ship *Columbia*, where I arrived January 21st. The night previous to our reaching Liverpool, we were nearly lost on Holyhead. We were running directly on to the land to the southward of the lighthouse, it blowing hard at the time from s. w., with much rain. All of a sudden it cleared up, and we caught sight of the light; and as soon as we had taking the bearings of it, the same bad weather came on again. It really appeared that the arm of Providence was stretched out here to save us; another quarter of an hour, and no one, perhaps, would have ever heard anything more of us, had we continued the course we were steering before we saw the light. Thank God! I have now returned safely to England from California. I thoroughly recommend no friend of mine to go there. What I had to go through is trifling to what many suffer, and you may rely upon it, that the reports from California about the large quantity of gold that leaves that country, are exaggerated. These reports are merely published to induce shippers to send their goods out, and nothing more. There is no doubt that much gold has been sent from thence; still, a very trifling quantity among 200,000 diggers. Even if there had been 50,000,000 dollars sent away during the last twelve months, as stated, that is only an average of £50 to each man who has been digging. When I left there, the merchants of San Francisco were indebted to the merchants here and in the States, 40,000,000 dollars for goods, which does not place that country in a very wholesome position. Those who are fond of sporting, may pass several months in that pursuit, the country being richly stocked with elk, deer, buffalo, bears, &c., &c., &c., and wild fowls in the greatest abundance. I have seen at least 1,000,000 of geese in one day, and one man often shoots from 25 to 30 in a day.

HAVING thus finished my Journal, and having to the best of my ability stated the real condition of the Pitcairn Islanders, I leave my readers to decide how far these poor, but truly good people deserve the notice of the British public. A large sum is subscribed annually in this country for Missionary purposes. Surely, these islanders have a claim for assistance either from this or similar charitable institutions.

In a pecuniary point of view much might be done in sending out clothing and other necessary comforts. It must be admitted that some three or four of the islanders, after coming from Tahiti, commenced distilling, and became intoxicated. Fortunately, that continued but a very short time. For 20 years these people have drunk nothing but water, except now and then a glass of wine, given then on board some of the vessels that have called at the island. But upon the whole it may be safely affirmed that, as a community, they are free from any of the vices incident to more civilized states, while their virtues and moral goodness are well worthy of our admiration and example.

LIST OF SHIPPING WHICH HAVE TOUCHED AT PITCAIRN'S ISLAND SINCE 1808.

Date.	Name of Vessel.	Where from.	Name of Captain.
1808	Topaz,	Boston,	Folger.
1814	H.M. Ships, Britain, Sir Thos. Staines, and Tagus.		
1823	Cyrus,	London,	J. Hall.
1824	Oneo,	Nantucket,	G. Worth.
"	Maryland,	Ditto,	O. Folger.
"	Waverly,	Oahu,	W. Dana.
1825	Waverly,	Ditto,	Ditto.
"	Melantho,	London,	N. Folger.
"	Luna,	Nantucket,	A. Swain.
"	H.M.S. Blossoms,		W. F. Beechy.
1826	Roscoe,	New Bedford,	G. Worth.
"	Gov. McQuarrie,		R. Brimmer.
"	Tahiti.		
"	Lovely Ann,	London,	P. Blythe.
1827	Resident,	Nantucket,	Winslow.
"	Connecticut,	Norwich,	Chester.
"	Discoverer,	Valparaiso,	Lindsey.
1828	Weymouth,	Nantucket,	M. Harris.
"	Discoverer,	Valparaiso,	Grimwood.
1829	Ganges,	Nantucket,	J. Coffin.
"	Voladoe,	Valparaiso,	J. Clarke.
"	Independence,	Nantucket,	Whippy.
"	Orion,	Ditto,	Alley.
"	Connecticut,	Norwich,	P. Smith.
"	Rob Roy,	Boston,	T. Percival.
"	Unity,		Madse.
1830	H.M.S. Seringapatam,		Waldegrave.
"	Nelson,	London,	E. David.
"	Courier de Bordeaux,		T. Maurac.
"	Eagle,	London,	J. Greave.
1831	Fabius,	Nantucket,	Coffin.
"	H.M.S. Comet, A.A.,		Sandilands.
"	Lucy Anne,	New S. Wales,	J. Curry.
"	Origon,	Fairhaven,	T. Delano.
"	Chas. Doggit,	Salem,	W. Driver.
"	Pomarre,	Valparaiso,	J. Clark.
1832	Carman,	Ditto,	A. Maurac.
"	Independence,	Nantucket,	Whippy.

Date.	Name of Vessel.	Where from.	Name of Captain.
1832	Maria,	Tahiti,	T. Ebriel.
,,	Alexander,	Nantucket,	S. Swain.
,,	Eagle,	London,	Grave.
1833	H.M.S. Challenger,		Fremantle.
,,	Albion,	Tahiti,	Johnson.
,,	Maria,	Ditto,	T. Ebriel.
,,	Russian Sloop of War,	America.	
,,	Ballance,	Rhode Island,	Dogget.
,,	Ploughboy,	Nantucket,	W. Chase.
1834	Tuscan,	London,	T. Staves.
,,	Olivia,	Boston,	C. Kendal.
,,	Olive Branch,	Tahiti,	Cornish.
,,	Olivia,	Boston,	C. Kendal.
1835	Phœnix,	New Bedford,	S. Sandford.
,,	Enterprize,	Ditto,	Winslow.
1836	Ann,	London,	R. Howe.
,,	Triton,	New Bedford,	Cavi.
,,	Phœnix,	Ditto,	Sandford.
,,	Columbo,	Boston,	Williams.
,,	Peruvian,	Ditto,	Sweetland.
,,	Fortune,	Ditto,	Upham.
,,	Polynesiana,	Valparaiso,	Maurice.
1837	H.M.S. Acteon,		Lord E. Russell.
,,	Colo Colo,	Chili,	Senorei.
,,	Hobomok,	Falmouth,	H. C. Bunker.
,,	H.M.S. Imogine,		H. W. Bruce.
1838	Alexander Coffin,	Nantucket,	Congdon.
,,	George,	Ditto,	Swain.
,,	Sapphire,	Salem,	H. H. Smith.
,,	Hobomok,	Falmouth,	Bunker.
,,	Polynesiana,	Valparaiso,	Maurice.
,,	Sapphire,	Salem,	H. H. Smith.
,,	Lady Amherst,	London,	W. Bushel.
,,	Kent,	Boston,	J. Steel.
,,	H.M.S. Fly,		R. Elliott.
,,	Ferdinand,	Havre.	
1839	John Cockrel,	Ditto,	R. Walsh.
,,	Thos. Williams,	Storrington,	P. Hall.
,,	Audley Clarke,	Bristol, R.I.,	Sherman.
,,	Christopher Mitchell,		Veeder.
,,	Logan,		Briggs.
,,	Ceres,	Wilmington.	
,,	Edward Agnes,		
,,	Cyrus,		Hussey.
,,	Pacific,		Palmer.
,,	Friends,	Valparaiso,	Rugg.

Date.	Name of Vessel.	Where from.	Name of Captain.
1839	Phœnix,	Nantucket,	Hussey.
,,	H.M.S. Sparrowhawk,		J. Shepherd.
,,	Alexander,	New Bedford,	C. Kelson.
,,	William Thompson,	Ditto,	E. Doane.
1840	Swift,	Ditto,	T. Toby.
,,	Cr. Rover Bride,	New S. Wales,	Biddulph.
,,	Bq. Folura,	Ditto,	Norris.
,,	Ann,	Nantucket,	P. C. Broach.
,,	Almira,	Edgartown,	Toby.
,,	S. Crusader,	Chili, to N.S.W.	P. Inglis.
,,	Camden, Missry. Brig,		Morgan.
,,	Persia,	New Bedford.	Norton.
,,	Mechanic,	Newport, R.I.	
1841	Christopher Mitchell,		Veerdon.
,,	Rose,	Nantucket,	B. A. Coleman.
,,	S. Elizabeth,	London,	J. E. Bunker.
,,	Alexander,	New Bedford.	
,,	S. Atlantic,	Nantucket.	
,,	Polynesiana.		
,,	Persia,	New Bedford,	Norton.
,,	S. Milo,	Ditto,	Gardner.
,,	S. Loan,		Merchant.
,,	Bq. Nelson,		S. D. Norris.
,,	,, Lady Raffles,	London,	H. Height.
,,	S. Europa,	Havre.	
,,	S. Navy,	New Bedford,	Brock.
,,	S. General Williams,	New London,	E. G. Bailey.
,,	H.M.S. Curaçoa,		J. Jones.
,,	S. Mechanic,	New Bedford,	S. Prout.
,,	Sr. La Rita,	Valparaiso,	Maurice.
,,	S. Erie,	Fairhaven,	P. Lucas.
,,	S. Splendid,	Edgartown,	T. E. Coffin.
,,	S. Cyrus,	Nantucket.	
,,	S. America,	Bristol, R.I.,	G. Richmond.
1842	S. Wm. Rotch,	New Bedford,	R. Toby.
,,	S. Orbet,	Nantucket,	J. Gardner.
,,	S. Barclay,	Nantucket,	P. Barney.
,,	S. Chas. Curran,	Ditto,	T. S. Swain.
,,	S. Mariner,	Ditto,	G. Palmer.
,,	S. General Washington,	Wareham,	C. C. Russell.
,,	S. General Williams,	New London,	E. G. Bailey.
,,	S. Zone,	Nantucket,	W. Hiller.
,,	S. Jefferson,		E. Coffin.
,,	S. Pacific,		W. Taber.
,,	S. London Packet,	Fairhaven.	
,,	S. Nancy,		T. Jay.

AND THE ISLANDERS. 245

Date.	Name of Vessel.	Where from.	Name of Captain.
1842	Bq. Franklin,	New Bedford,	W. Beetle.
,,	S. Japan,	Nantucket,	B. Riddle.
,,	S. Atlantic,	Ditto,	G. C. Hog.
,,	Columbus Gardner,	Ditto,	W. B. Gardner.
,,	Lydia Cathcart,	Ditto.	
,,	S. Clematis,	New London,	G.G. Benjamins
,,	S. Chris. Mitchell,		Keen.
,,	S. General Washington.		
,,	Bq. George,	Storrington,	J. B. Forsett.
,,	S. Metsoom,	New Bedford,	J. Reynolds.
,,	Bq. Alto,	Fairhaven,	J. W. Coffin.
,,	S. Nelson,	New S. Wales,	W. Roggers.
,,	S. Ceres,	Wilmington,	Ayers.
,,	Bq. Charles,	London,	R. Hammer.
,,	S. Kingston,	Nantucket,	W. Pearson.
,,	S. Samuel Robertson,	New Bedford,	Warren.
,,	S. Nile,	Ditto,	Cook.
,,	S. Chili,	Ditto,	D. B. Delane.
1843	S. Mariner,		G. Palmer.
,,	S. Charles,	New Bedford,	R. Gardner.
,,	S. Friendship,		S. Taber.
,,	S. Rose,		B. Swain.
,,	S. Swift,	New Bedford,	Fisher,
,,	S. Splendid.		
,,	S. South Carolina,	Ede. town,	E. Coffin.
,,	H.M.S. Talbot,		Sir F. Thompson
,,	S. Lioncourt,	Havre,	T. Howe.
,,	Bq. Carnarvon,	New S. Wales.	
,,	S. Marcia,	Fairhaven,	E. Washer.
,,	S. Balance,	Providence,	D. H. Reed.
,,	S. Eagle,	New Bedford,	E. H. Coffin.
,,	Bq. Mercury,	New Bedford,	Haskell.
,,	Bq. America.		
,,	S. Content.		
,,	S. Gen. Washington,	Nantucket,	C. C. Russell.
,,	Bq. Drimo,	Sippican,	C. Hammond.
,,	S. Kingston,		W. Rawson.
,,	S. Metrion,	New Bedford,	Reynolds.
,,	S. Eliza Adams,	Fairhaven,	W. Holly.
,,	S. Mariner,	Nantucket.	
,,	S. General Washington,	Wareham,	C. C. Russell.
,,	S. Clarkson,	Nantucket.	
,,	Sr. Sagaz,		R. Griggs.
,,	S. Kutusoff,	New Bedford,	H. Cox.
,,	S. Rose,		W. B. Swain.
,,	Bq. America.		

Date.	Name of Vessel.	Where from.	Name of Captain.
1844	S. Thames,	Sagharbour,	J. R. Bishop.
,,	Metacom,		J. Reynolds.
,,	S. Nancy,	Havre,	T. Jay.
,,	S. George,	Fairhaven,	J. H. Swift.
,,	Bq. Sir J. Byng,		M. Megget.
,,	S. Eleanor,	London,	W. Barnett.
,,	S. Mercury,	New Bedford.	
,,	S. Clarkson,	Nantucket,	J. C. Chase.
,,	Bq. Jules,	Rosville.	
,,	S. Altreoida.		
,,	S. Isaac Howland,	New Bedford,	L. Fisher.
,,	Bq. Cherokee,	Ditto,	W. Devoe.
,,	S. Lowell,	New London,	G.G. Benjamins
,,	S. John Adams,		Thompson.
,,	H.M.S. Basilisk,		H. Hunt.
,,	S. Clarkson.		
,,	S. Almica.		
,,	S. Rose,		W. B. Swain.
1845	S. William Baker,	Warren,	Bowden.
,,	S. Franklin,	Sagharbour.	
,,	S. Splendid,	Cold Spring.	
,,	S. John Mills,	Sagharbour,	J. M. Hedges.
,,	S. Mary Anne,	New London,	G. Destin.
,,	S. Phœnix,	New Bedford,	P. Butler.
,,	S. Argo,	Nantes,	Grandaing.
,,	S. Huntress,	New Bedford,	E. Sherman.
,,	S. Hudson,	Sagharbour,	Henry.
,,	S. Albion.		
,,	Brunswick,	New Bedford,	King.
,,	Philip West,	Green Pt.	I. S. Case.
,,	S. Henry Luke,	Warren,	H. Champion.
,,	S. Joseph Heydon,	Bremen,	Parker.
,,	S. Champion,		J. S. Sandford.
,,	S. Julian,	New Bedford,	Blackneer.
,,	S. Messenger,	Ditto.	
,,	Ontario,	Nantucket,	Gibbs.
,,	S. Fabius,		Nickerson.
,,	S. Lexington,	Nantucket,	Weeks.
,,	S. Thomas Dickason,		Lowen.
,,	S. Sarah Francis,		Gardner.
,,	S. Alexander,		J. R. Darrin.
,,	Bg. Eliza,	French Govrnt.	
,,	S. Planter,		B. J. Folger.
,,	S. Rose,		W. B. Swain.
1846	S. Minerva,		Smally.
,,	Bq. Pacific,	Fairhaven,	Alder.

Date.	Name of Vessel.	Where from.	Name of Captain.
1846	S. Eliza,	L. B. Jemmy,	J. Church.
,,	S. Levi Starback,	Nantucket,	Moses.
,,	S. Marcus,		S. H. Faber.
,,	S. Carolina,	French Govrnt.	
,,	S. John Adams,	New Bedford,	Wilcox.
,,	Huntsville,		Howe.
,,	Bq. Pacific,	Fairhaven,	Alder.
,,	Nantathel,	New London,	Smith.
,,	Kutusoff,	New Bedford,	Shokley.
,,	S. Rowan,	Ditto.	
,,	S. Henry Lee,	Sagharbour.	
,,	S. Eleanor.		
,,	S. Friend,	Green Pt.	
,,	S. Enterprize,	New Bedford,	S. Braytore.
,,	S. Clematine,	Ditto.	
,,	S. Comet,	Storrington,	J. Bolter.
,,	S. General Williams,	New London,	J. Ward.
,,	S. Governor Troop.		
,,	S. Hannibal,	New London,	J. C. Brooks.
,,	S. Archer,	New Bedford,	M. Suell.
,,	S. Isaac Howland,		Covry.
,,	S. Pioneer.		
,,	S. Ontario.		
,,	S. Champion.		
,,	S. William Hamilton,	New Bedford,	L. Fisher.
,,	S. St. George,	Ditto,	G. W. Sloman.
,,	Bq. Phleretus.		
,,	S. Montpelier,		Taber.
,,	S. Harvest,	Nantucket,	Coffin.
,,	S. Roscoe,		E. M. Cleave.
,,	S. Mary,	Nantucket,	C. Pitman.
,,	S. Henry Clay,		Auster.
,,	S. Messenger,	New Bedford.	
,,	Morris,	Falmouth.	
,,	S. Charles Carroll.		
,,	S. General Scott,	New London,	W. Bushell.
,,	S. Washington,	Nantucket,	G. Palmer.
,,	S. Lion of Bordeaux,	Rio Janeiro,	F. Howland.
,,	S. Java,	Fairhaven,	D. Lucas.
,,	S. Balam,	New Bedford,	C. Dater.
,,	S. General Washington,	Wareham,	C. Russell.
,,	S. Arnolda,	New Bedford,	Coffin.
,,	Alexander Barclay,	Bremen,	Fish.
,,	S. Enterprise,	Nantucket,	S. C. Wyer.
,,	S. Harvest.		
,,	S. Henry Clay,	Nantucket,	E. C. Austin.

Date.	Name of Vessel.	Where from.	Name of Captain.
1847	S. Nantucket,	Nantucket,	C. Gardner.
,,	H.M.S. Spy,		Woodbridge.
,,	S. Richard Mitchell,	Nantucket,	C. Long.
,,	S. Martha,	Ditto,	H. B. Folger.
,,	S. William Hamilton,	New Bedford.	L. Fisher.
,,	S. Francis,	Ditto,	S. Pannington.
,,	Bq. Bayard,	Green Pt.,	Fordham.
,,	Solomon Salters,	Fallriver.	
,,	S. Hope,	Providence.	
,,	S. Pacific,	New Bedford.	
,,	S. Three Brothers,	Nantucket,	J. Mitchell.
,,	S. Navigator,	Ditto.	
,,	S. Isaac Howland.		
,,	Bq. Sarah.		
,,	Bq. Iris,	New London,	W. C. Haynes.
,,	Bq. Antenon.		
1848	S. Harvest,		G. C. Coffin.
,,	Falcon,		Kirby.
,,	Mancke,		A. Gibbs.
,,	H.M.S. Calypso,		Worth.
,,	Sr. Caupolicon.		
,,	S. Martha,	Newport,	Gifford.
,,	S. Margaret Scott,	New Bedford,	Lucas.
,,	William Nicoll,	London,	W. Bushell.
,,	S. Washington,	Nantucket,	S. Bailey.
1849	S. Herald,	New Bedford,	A. Malcomb.
,,	Dover,	New London,	C. Jeffrey.
,,	S. General Scott,	Ditto,	G. C. Harris.
,,	S. Tuscanora,	Cold Spring,	S. Leek.
,,	S. Ontario,	Sagharbour,	W. Payne.
,,	Bg. Kirkwood,	Nantucket,	C. C. Jolly.
,,	Bg. Fanny,	Auckland,	Leathart.
,,	H.M.S. Pandora,		T. Wood.
,,	Sr. Bandicoot,	V. Diemen's L.	Carraway.
,,	H.M.S. Daphne,		Fanshawe.
,,	Sr. Union,	New S. Wales,	Milne.
,,	Bq. Elizabeth Archer,	Ditto,	Cobb.
,,	Bq. Dunbarton,	New Bedford,	Mayhew.
,,	Sr. Vansittart,	V. Diemen's L.	J. Gill.
,,	S. William Nicol,	London,	Wm. Bushell.
,,	Sr. Frederick,	Auckland,	H. Joseph.
,,	Sr. Agenoria,	V. Diemen's L.	Martin.
,,	Bq. David Malcolm,	Ditto,	Smith.
,,	Bg. Georgiana,	San Francisco,	F. Page.
,,	Bq. Pilgrim,	Auckland,	Frances.
1850	S. Meteor,		Turner.

Date.	Name of Vessel.	Where from.	Name of Captain.
1850	S. Phœnix,	New Bedford,	J. M. Cleave.
,,	Bq. Dryad,	Ditto,	S. C. Fisher.
,,	S. Henry Clay,		J. Skinner.
,,	Bq. Margaret Brock,	V. Diemen's L.	M'Mechan.
,,	Sr. Rose,	New S. Wales,	Patterson.
,,	Bq. Noble,	Auckland,	H. Parker.
,,	S. George and Susan,	New Bedford,	White.
,,	Bq. Colonist,	Adelaide,	J. Marshall.

TOTAL NUMBER OF VESSELS, 322.

S. *for Ship.* | Bq. *for Barque.* | Bg. *for Brig.*
Sr. *for Schooner.* | Cr. *for Cutter.*

As the Author intends to remit a portion of the profits arising from the sale of this work to the islanders, who are very scantily provided with clothing and other necessary comforts, parties who wish to give a small donation to this virtuous little community, may (by taking more copies than they require for their own use) send the spare ones to the islanders themselves *through the Author*. As every stranger calling at Pitcairn's Island is too glad to procure some memento of them, a book containing a full description of these islanders, would sell to strangers visiting the island, to greater advantage than anything else; and it would not only do them much good in a pecuniary point of view, but would place their present unfortunate condition more fully before the public, now more than ever needed.

LIST OF SUBSCRIBERS.

	Copies.	Copies for the Isldrs.
Addington, H. U., Esq., 78, Eaton Place	2	2
Admiralty Library, Whitehall	1	0
Alexander, J., Miss	1	0
Attree, Hooper, Esq., 9, Cavendish Street	1	0
Avery, J., Miss	1	0
Ayerst, Francis, Limehouse	1	0
Burlington, Right Hon. Earl of, Compton Place	4	0
Bell, Lady	1	0
Barrow, John, Esq., Admiralty, Whitehall	2	0
Baxter, —, Esq.	1	0
Baxter, Rev. W., The Cottage, Cheltenham	1	0
Barnet, Dr., 34, Chesham Place	1	0
Bates, J., Esq.	1	0
Barford, A. H., Esq., 1, Cornwall Terrace	1	0
Batt, J. A., Esq.	1	0

LIST OF SUBSCRIBERS. 251

	Copies.	Copies for the Isldrs.
Barber, Geo., Esq., Horsham	1	0
Beechy, Capt. F. W., R. N., 8, Westbourne Crescent	1	4
Benson, Capt. H. M., 66th Regt.	1	0
Bent, H., Esq.	1	0
Bell, Mrs., Whitehaven	1	0
Bell, —, Esq. ,,	1	0
Benson, Mrs. ,,	1	0
Benson, Miss ,,	1	0
Blair, W., Esq., 53, Margaret Street, Cavendish Square	1	0
Blake, Colonel, 56, Regency Square, Brighton	1	0
Boyd, Major-General, Exeter	1	0
Boyd, M., Esq., 4, Bank Buildings, London.	1	0
Booth, Mrs.	1	0
Boyer, Hext, Esq.	1	0
Booth, Rev. R., Radmill Rectory, Lewes	1	0
Bonsor, J., Esq., Salisbury Square	1	0
Brown, Mrs., 22, Bloombury Square	2	0
Brown, John, Esq.	1	0
Bown, J. A., Esq., Eastbourne	1	0
Brocklebank, Miss, Whitehaven	1	0
Brockbank, —, Esq. ,,	1	0
Browning, Henry, Esq.	1	0
Brodie, Mrs., The Gore, Eastbourne	0	12
Brodie, Miss ,,	2	0
Brodie, J., Miss ,,	2	0
Brodie, L., Miss ,,	2	0
Brodie, W., Esq. ,,	1	0
Brodie, A., Esq., 5, Cavendish Square	7	7
Brodie, F., Esq., Esher	5	0
Burrow, Miss, Whitehaven	3	0
Burrow, E., Miss, Welling	1	0
Burrow, A. A., Esq.	1	0
Burrow, A., Mrs.	1	0
Butcher, Mrs., Epsom	1	0
Burgess, Rev. W. G.	2	0
Burn, Miss, Whitehaven	1	0
Buschman, 32, Brunswick Terrace	1	0
Canning, Viscountess, 10, Grosvenor Square	1	0

252 LIST OF SUBSCRIBERS.

	Copies.	Copies for the Isldrs.
Cremorne, Dowager Lady, 3, Great Stanhope Street.	1	0
Cranworth, Lady	1	0
Cavendish, Hon. Mrs., 1, Belgrave Square . .	1	0
Cavendish, Hon. R., 1, Belgrave Square . . .	2	0
Capper, Miss, Upper Dicker, Horsbridge . .	2	0
Cassius, —, Esq., 36, Newman Street, Oxford Street.	1	0
Caarten, Miss	1	0
Carden, James, Esq., Burton, Westmoreland . .	5	0
Carden, R. W., Esq., Sheriff and Alderman . .	6	0
Carpenter, Mrs., 45, Brunswick Square, Brighton .	1	0
Chamberlyn, Miss	1	0
Charlwood, Colonel	1	0
Charlton, Rev. C. W., Laughton . . .	1	0
Chamber, Dr., 65, Harley Street	1	0
Chamber, G. F., Esq.	1	0
Charrington, the Misses, Tonbridge Wells . .	1	1
Charrington, F., Esq., Mile-end . . .	1	1
Chadwick, H. M., Esq., New Hall, Sutton Coldfield .	2	2
Charleton, Mrs., Chilwell Hall, Nottingham . .	2	0
Childes, Mrs. William, 16, Eaton Square . . .	3	0
Church, —, Esq., Leamington . . .	1	0
Christie, Mrs., Thornthwaite, Keswick . . .	1	0
Clark, Sir James, Bart.	1	0
Clark, W. R., Esq., 17, Saville Row . . .	1	0
Clark, Dr., Colchester	1	0
C. H.	1	0
C. R.	1	0
Cook, Miss, 18, Clarence Square, Brighton . .	1	0
Cole, Mr.	1	0
Collins, F., Esq., Clapham . . .	1	0
Constable, Mrs., Ringmer, Sussex . . .	1	0
Cormack, — Esq., 6, Percy Street, Bedford Square .	1	0
Cooper, Rev. George, Bilmington, Sussex . .	1	0
Cook, Esq., Dawsbury, Yorkshire . . .	1	0
Cotterill, Rev. S. W.	1	0
Conworth, J., Esq.	1	0
Crawford, Mrs., Camberwell	1	0
Cutler, Miss, Exeter.	1	0
Curwood, Capel, Esq., 1, Doughty Street . .	6	0
Cochrane, Admiral Sir Thomas, 33, Belgrave Square	1	0

LIST OF SUBSCRIBERS. 253

	Copies.	Copies for the Isldrs.
De la Ware, The Countess of	3	0
Ducie, Viscountess, 24, Belgrave Square	6	0
Dundas, Lady Emily	1	0
Domville, Sir W., Bart.	2	4
Dalzel, —, Esq., 36, Russell Square, Brighton	1	0
Davidson, D. W., Esq., 65, Harley Street	1	0
Davidson, Miss	1	0
Dixon, Miss	1	0
Dixon, Rev. George, 16, Chester Terrace, Eaton Square	1	0
Doxat, Mrs. Lewes, 43, Harley Street	1	0
Darby, Miss, 5, New Street, Spring Gardens	2	0
Durrant, Mrs., Ipswich	8	0
Erskine, Right Hon. Lord	1	0
Eden, —, Esq., Admiralty, Somerset House	1	0
Edgeworth, Mrs., 1, Chesham Place, Hastings	2	0
Elwood, Colonel, Clayton Priory, Sussex	1	0
Elwood, Mrs., Clayton Priory, Sussex	1	0
Enys, Mrs. Enys, Cornwall	2	0
Ewart, H., Esq., 7, Duchess Street, Portland Place	2	0
Falkner, Rev. W. B.	1	0
Ferrand, Mrs., Tunstall, Suffolk	3	0
Ferner, J., Esq., 3, Minories	10	0
Ferrar, Eastbourne, Esq., 57, Tower	1	0
Field, J., Esq.	1	0
Fisher, Robert, Esq., Gresham Club	1	0
Fletcher, Mrs., Leamington	1	0
Fletcher, Miss, Leamington	1	0
Folthorpe, Esq., Library, North Street, Brighton	1	0
Foljomb, Mrs., Leamington	1	0
Foster, Mrs., 45, Upper Rathmines, Dublin	1	0
Fisher, Abraham, Esq., Seatoller, Keswick	4	0
Fisher, J. C., Esq., Woodhall, Cockermouth	1	0
Fisher, Miss, Thornthwaite, Keswick	1	0
Fishwick, Miss	6	0
Freeman, Mrs., Leamington War.	1	2
Freeman, Mrs. Spencer, Leamington War.	1	0
Fraseir, Miss, Eastbourne	1	0

254   LIST OF SUBSCRIBERS.

	Copies.	Copies for the Isldrs.
Frances, —, Esq., Admiralty, Somerset House	1	0
Friend, Eastbourne	2	0
Friend	1	0
Friend, Edinburgh	8	0
Friend, Whitehaven	1	0
Friend, Whitehaven	1	0
Friend, Chelsea	1	0
Fraser, Patrick, 62, Guildford Street	1	0
Fraser, Rev. P., 18, New Street, Spring Gardens	2	2
Fussell, Thomas, Esq., Wadbury House, Frome	6	0
Fussell, T. S. D., Esq., Great Elm, Frome	5	0
Gordon, Her Grace the Duchess of, Huntley Lodge	1	3
Grabowski, Countess, 83, Baker Street, Portman Square	1	0
Gann, A., Esq., Crosby Square	1	0
Gell, J. H., Esq., Lewes	1	0
Gell, J., Esq., Lewes	1	0
Gell, Miss E., Lewes	1	0
Gell, Rev. J. P., 16, Upper Seymour Street, Portman Square	1	0
Gibbs, G., Esq., Horse Guards, Whitehall	1	0
Gilbert, J. D., Esq., Trelisick, Cornwall	1	0
Gilbert, Miss, Eastbourne	2	0
Gibson, Miss, Thornthwaite, Keswick	1	0
Gower, Miss, 20, York Terrace, Regent's Park	1	0
Goldie, Mrs., 34, Melville Street, Edinburgh	5	0
Gosden, Mr., Eastbourne	1	0
Goldsmith, —, Esq., Admiralty, Somerset House	1	0
Good, Miss, 46, Burton Crescent	1	0
Goodman, Rev. George, 120, Salisbury Square	1	0
Gledstaines, J. H., Esq., 3, White Lion Court	1	0
Grace, Mrs., Wardrobe, Bucks	4	0
Graham, Mrs., The Hall, Clapham	4	0
Gwynne, Mrs., 16, Hyde Park Square	1	3
Grove, Miss	3	0
Hall, Dr., Eastbourne	1	0
Hannah, Dr., 4, Pavilion Parade, Brighton	1	0
Hart, F., Esq., 11, Stanhope Place, Hyde Park	4	0

LIST OF SUBSCRIBERS. 255

	Copies.	Copies for the Isldrs.
Haywood, T. C., Esq.	1	0
Hawkins, Geo., Esq.	1	0
Hartshorne, Miss, East Retford, Notts	1	0
Hancock, Miss, Camden Grove, Kensington	1	0
Harrison, C. H. R., Esq., 13, Landsdown Road	4	0
Harrison, Mrs., Whitehaven	1	0
Harrison, G. E., Esq., Mornington Crescent	1	0
Hastings, Mrs., 14, Albemarle Street	1	0
Hellyer, Mrs.	2	0
Hellyer, Mrs. W.	1	0
Hellyer, Rev. Hugh	1	0
Haywood, S., Esq.	1	0
Hill, Rev. A. L.	1	0
Holmes, Mrs., Eastbourne	2	0
Hood, W. C., Esq., 64, Westbourne Terrace	6	0
Hood, Mrs. W. C., 64, Westbourne Terrace	2	0
Hood, William, jun., Esq., 109, Gloucester Terrace	1	0
Hood, Mrs. William, 109, Gloucester Terrace	1	0
Hood, Walter, Esq., Gloucester Terrace	4	0
Hooper, —, Esq., Admiralty, Somerset House	1	0
Hooper, Miss, Bloomsbury Square	1	0
Hoper, Rev. H., Portslade Vicarage, Brighton	1	0
Hobson, Meade, Esq., Exeter	1	0
Hobson, Jesse, Esq.	1	0
Huth, Mr. C. F., 25, Upper Harley Street	2	0
Huth, Miss, 33, Upper Harley Street	1	0
Hurlock, Dr., 5, Hanover Crescent, Brighton	1	0
H. E. M., Colchester	1	0
Humphries, Mrs., 8, South Bank, Regent's Park	4	0
Harborow, Mrs., 38, Argyle St., King's Cross	2	0
Hannington, Mrs. C. S., West Street, Brighton	1	0
Hope, Rev. R., 38, Charter House Square	1	0
James, Mrs., 7, Richmond Place, Brighton	1	0
Ibbetson, Mrs., 34, Chester Terrace, Regent's Park	2	0
Ibbetson, Captain, A. D. C., 3, Circus Road, St. John's Wood	1	0
Ibbetson, Henry, Esq., 34, Chester Terrace	1	0
James, Robert, Esq., Hampstead	4	0
Jemmet, Miss, 4, Marine Square, Brighton	1	0

256   LIST OF SUBSCRIBERS.

	Copies.	Copies for the Isldrs.
Johnson, Mrs., Eastbourne	1	0
Jones, Esq., Whitehaven	1	0
Jones, Mrs. C. W., Leamington	1	0
Knox, Rev. H. C., Lechlade Rectory, Gloucestershire	4	0
Kitchenor, Mrs., 14, Wilton Place, Belgrave Square	1	0
Knight, James, Esq.	1	0
Long, Lady Catherine, Eastbourne	1	0
Leeds, Lady, Ryde, Isle of Wight	1	0
Lanyon, Charles, Esq., Donegal Square, Belfast	6	0
Landon, E. W., Esq., 2, St. Margaret's Hill	1	0
Lamb, H., Esq., Salisbury Square	1	0
Lay, Miss, Eastbourne	1	0
Laurie, C., Esq., Sydenham, Kent	4	0
Leeds, Augustus, Esq., Ryde, Isle of Wight	1	0
Lee, Major, Exeter	1	0
Legget, L.	1	0
Lindsey, Mrs. Basil	1	0
Library, Eastbourne	1	0
Loft, Miss, 3, Castle Place, Hastings	1	0
Lorie, Dr., 30, Westbourne Terrace	2	0
M'Donnell, Lieutenant-General	1	2
Madely, Geo., Esq., Warwick Square, Kensington	1	0
Mason, Mrs., Budleigh Salterton, Exeter	1	0
Mangeon, A., Esq., Southampton	1	0
Martin, Mrs., Lower Grosvenor Street	4	0
Marsh, Rev. William, D.D., Leamington	1	1
Mangles, F., Esq.	1	0
Mangles, R. D., Esq., East India House	1	0
M'Laren, A. C., Esq.	1	0
M'Lean, John, M.D.	1	0
Meineitzhagen, Mrs., 28, Devonshire Place	2	0
Melhuish, Mrs., 29, St. Swithin's Lane	2	0
Menzies, Mrs., Eastbourne	1	0
Mortimer, Miss, Eastbourne	4	0
Morrice, Mrs., 29, Pulteney Street, Bath	2	0
Morrice, Miss M., Pulteney Street, Bath	1	0
Morrice, Rev. W. D., Westbury	1	0

LIST OF SUBSCRIBERS.

	Copies.	Copies for the Isldrs.
Morrice, J. W., Esq., 11, Hyde Park Square	1	0
Mowatt, Miss, 18, York Terrace	1	0
Moneypenny, —, Esq., Saint Andrew's, Fifeshire	1	1
M'Whinney, Mrs., 5, Upper Brunswick Place, Brighton	1	0
Neave, Miss, Royal Hospital, Chelsea	1	0
Newbury, Captain, 5, Camden Grove, Kensington	1	0
Nesbit, Mrs.	1	0
Noel, Rev. Zealand, Leamington	2	0
O'Conner, Mrs., 4 Sussex Place, Southampton	1	0
Ogle, Mrs., Eastbourne	2	0
Orr, Mrs., 16, Westbourne Place, Chelsea	1	0
Owen, Professor Richard, Royal College of Surgeons.	2	0
Parr, Rev. T., Westbury Rectory, Shropshire	2	0
Patten, Mrs., Bishop's Hull House, Taunton	6	0
Perry, Mrs., Whitehaven	1	0
Perry, Miss, New Courthouse, Cheltenham	2	0
Phillips, Miss	1	0
Pitman, Rev. Thos., Eastbourne	3	0
Pierpoint, Rev. R. W., Eastbourne	1	0
Pelham, F., Eastbourne	1	0
Pigou, Miss, Amhurst Place, Guernsey	1	0
Podmore, C., Esq.	6	0
Powncett, Rothwell, Esq.	1	0
Preston, Mrs., Folkington House, Sussex	2	0
Ponsonby, Miss., Whitehaven	1	0
Pollock, Mrs., 19, Essex Street, Strand	2	0
Roxburgh, Dowager Duchess of, Her Grace	1	2
Roxburgh, Duke of, His Grace, Fleurs Castle	3	0
Roxburgh, Duchess of, Her Grace, Fleurs Castle	3	0
Rawdon, Colonel, M.P., 3, Great Stanhope Street	1	0
R. J. H.	1	0
Raines, Mrs. E., Easthoathly, Sussex	2	0
Ranken, Robert, Esq., M.D., Hastings	1	0
Radford, Mrs., 16, Eaton Square	1	0
Repton, Mrs., Cloisters, Westminster	1	0
Reid, Miss, 4, Cornwall Terrace	1	0

258   LIST OF SUBSCRIBERS.

	Copies.	Copies for the Isldrs.
Rendal, F. M., Esq., 8, Great George Street	1	0
Richards, Mrs., Eastbourne	1	0
Richardson, Capt., Sutton Hurst	2	0
Riley, Edward, Esq.	6	0
Robertson, Mrs., Ednam House, Kelso	3	6
Robinson, Miss E., Eastbourne	1	0
Roe, Major, 6, Marine Square, Brighton	1	0
Roberts, Dr., 75, Grand Parade	1	0
Russell, Mrs., Warneford House, Leamington	4	0
Sterling, Lady Caroline	1	0
Sawkins, Miss, 3, York Terrace	2	0
Scott, Hon. Mrs. Scott, 43, Pall Mall	1	0
Savell, H., Esq., 51, Old Broad Street	1	0
Saunders, Miss, Wandsworth	1	0
Shipton, W. E., Esq., 13, Prince's Row, Pimlico	1	0
Shernon, Mrs., Whitehaven	1	0
Shears, Daniel, Esq.	6	0
Shears, Daniel, Mrs.	1	0
Shears, Miss.	1	0
Shears, L. A., Esq.	1	0
Shears, D. F., Esq.	1	0
Shears, Mrs.	2	0
Shears, C., Esq., Walton, Suffolk	1	0
Shears, Wm., Esq., Lambeth	4	0
Shillinglaw, John, Esq., Chatham Place, Bridge St.	6	0
Skipsey, Mrs., 6, Middle Street, Brighton	1	0
Spencer, Mrs., Whitehaven	1	0
Stewart, A. B., Esq., Chapel House, Whitehaven	1	0
Stokes, Rev. G., Eastbourne	1	0
Stephen, Rev. W., Bledlow, Bucks.	1	0
Stringer, Miss, Gaudhurst, Kent	2	0
Stephenson, —, Esq.	2	0
Stockley, Capt. W. S., Tokenhouse Yard	1	0
Stride, Mrs., St. Martin's Hill, Dover	2	0
Strutt, H. M., Esq., 11, Ampton Place, Mecklingburg Square	1	0
Stafford, Mrs., 64, Montpelicr Road, Brighton	1	0
Simpkinson, Rev. J. M., Harrow	1	0
Simpson, Mrs., Southampton	1	0

LIST OF SUBSCRIBERS.   259

	Copies.	Copies for the Isldrs.
Stone, Mr. R. B., Eastbourne	1	0
Swift, Richard	1	0
Talbot, Hon. Mrs.	1	0
Thomas, Hon. Mrs.	1	3
Taylor, Rev. J. W. A., New Courthouse, Cheltenham	1	0
Thomas, Mrs. E.	1	0
ʼnorley, Mrs., Colchester	1	0
ιorley, Miss C., Colchester	1	0
relawney, Mrs., 7, New Steyne, Brighton	2	0
Tyler, Rev. J. E., 18, Bedford Square	1	0
Tucker, S., Esq., Welling	1	0
Turner, Sir E. Page, Bart., 22, Westbourne Street	1	0
Twiss and Browning, Mark Lane	2	0
Upperton, Mrs., 7, Landsdowne Place, Brighton	1	0
Walter, Mrs., Bear Wood, Berkshire	6	0
Walter, John, Esq., M.P., 40, Upper Grosvenor St.	6	0
Walter, —, Mrs., 40, Upper Grosvenor Street	4	0
Walter, H., Esq., 68, Russell Square	4	0
Walter, H., Mrs., 68, Russell Square	2	0
Walter, Capt. E., 8th Hussars	1	1
Walters, Mrs., 156, Albany Street	1	0
Walker, Mrs. Robertson, Whitehaven	1	0
Watt, J. D., Esq., Leamington	1	0
Watson, Rev. H., Jevington, Sussex	1	0
Ward, W.	1	0
Watkin, Edward, Esq., Secretary, Euston Sq. Station	1	0
Watson, Dr., Henrietta Street	1	0
Walsh, Rev. —.	1	0
Webb, H. B. M., Esq., Gresham Club	2	0
Wenkworth, Thos., Esq.	1	0
Winstaneley, Edward, Jun., 7, Poultry	1	0
Wilcox, Mrs., Dover	1	0
Wildman, Miss, Eastbourne	2	0
Willand, Major N., Eastbourne	1	0
Willand, Mrs. N., Eastbourne	1	0
Willand, Capt. L., Eastbourne	1	0
Willand, Mrs. L., Eastbourne	1	0

LIST OF SUBSCRIBERS.

	Copies.	Copies for the Isldrs.
Willson, Dr., 43, Clarence Square, Brighton	1	0
Whitfield, Mrs., Lewes	1	0
Wood, Mrs. W. Page	1	0
Wolrige, Mrs. Col., Reading	3	0
Wollaston, Miss	1	0
Young, Rev. James, Heathfield, Sussex.	1	0

The Author would feel obliged if his subscribers would pay for the several copies of this work which they have kindly taken, to *William* Brodie, Esq., by an order through the Post Office, Eastbourne, Sussex.

www.ingramcontent.com/pod-product-compliance
Lightning Source LLC
Chambersburg PA
CBHW021837220426
43663CB00005B/286